KERB 23

Journal of Landscape Architecture

2015

Kerb is published annually by Actar Publishers.

ISBN 978-1-940291-76-5
ISSN 1324-8049

Disclaimer
The opinions expressed in **Kerb** Issue 23 are those of the authors and are not endorsed by the edtorial team or RMIT University.

Each edition of **Kerb** is produced by a new student editorial team.

Editors
Georgia Aldous
Sophia Horomidis
Rebecca Pike
Robert Williamson

Editorial Board
Rosalea Monacella - **Kerb** 23 Supervisor
Bridget Keane, Liam Young, Mason White, Lola Sheppard, Luis Callejas.

Production Consultants
Marianne Dela Roza - **Kerb** 23 Transcriber
Frances Madigan - **Kerb** 23 Copy Editor

Art Direction
Sean Hogan - Trampoline Design.

Graphic Design
A collaboration between the editors and Sean Hogan - Trampoline Design.
trampoline.net.au

Acknowledgments
The editors would like to thank everyone involved in the production of the journal for their generous assistance and support during the process of this publication.

For orders, advertising and all other enquires contact:
ActarD Inc.

New York
355 Lexington Avenue, 8th Floor
New York, NY 10017
Phone: +1 212 966 2207
Fax: +1 212 966 2214
Email: salesnewyork@actar-d.com

Barcelona
Roca i Batlle 2
08023 Barcelona
Phone: +34 933 282 183
Email: eurosales@actar-d.com

www.actar-d.com

ACTAR

LANDSCAPE ARCHITECTURE
RMIT UNIVERSITY

RMIT UNIVERSITY

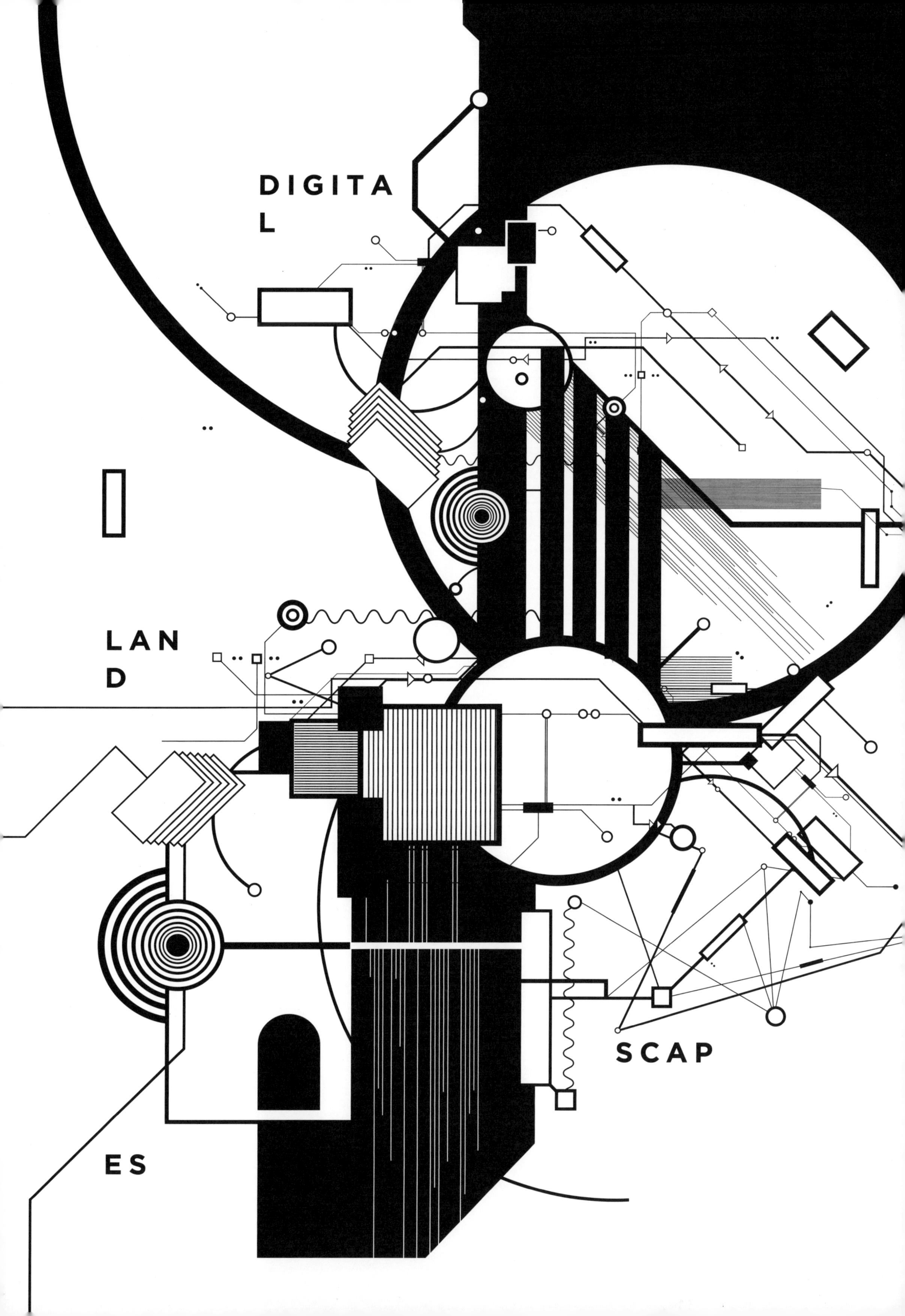
DIGITA
L
LAN
D
SCAP
ES

SELF REGULATORY

HUMAN DRIVEN

IDENTIFICATION

■ **Digital Ecologies**

● **Simulation**

◥ **Fabrication**

◣ **Augmentation**

DIGITAL LANDSCAPES

GEORGIA ALDOUS
SOPHIA HOROMIDIS
REBECCA PIKE
ROBERT WILLIAMSON

Digital Landscapes is the ecology that is driven by, and drives the alterations that are reflected by the landscape. The alterations on the built environment are the translation and manipulation of information and matter where the interaction between the physical and the digital drives the landscape's behavioural qualities as matter forms and reforms. The landscape is positioned not as material ground but as an ecology, an assemblage of interacting layers, often remaining latent, waiting to be discovered and decoded. Thomas Mical explores how each location is an 'array'; a space of innumerable behavioural variations that assume the possibility or impossibility of successfully employing design processes to augment the reflection on the landscape. This approach to the ground is also reflected in the digital landscape that it parallels; as Joe WT Scott notes, '[we experience] the real fear of the infinite in a world we rely on, yet we only glimpse the polished surface of via a screen.'

The surface is the outcome of constant evolution of matter and material that makes up the layers of the landscape: consequently, the landscape emerges from the digital landscape's ongoing adjustments that maintain balance between 'chance and control'. Scott likens layers of matter forming and reforming to the sublime. These layers show a vast and fearfully endless landscape that has infinite possibilities, and represent a resource for inventing our world without the stagnant matter and materials we reuse. However, Bradley Cantrell and Justine Holzman argue that this exploration of two distinct spaces – virtual and reality – is becoming invalid. Digital and landscape are no longer separate resources. They move us on from associating the digital with technology, and usher us towards the idea of a new perspective on digital landscapes.

As both physical and digital continue to alter and evolve into each other, Rod Barnett infers that we can only properly attempt to understand the change as we develop modes of interaction through the necessity of invention. This stems from the need to not only improve, but invent better quality of life, which comprehensively, reorients design informs design. In this way, substance and form are brought about through recognition of matter yet to be decoded.

Substances are nothing other than formed matters. Forms imply codes, modes of coding and decoding.[1]

In landscape architecture, identifying matter is linked to simulation. Two main forms of simulation arise: 'Identification of Idea' and 'Identification of Information'. In Experiencing Information, datum-visualisation introduces us to the literal imposition of data onto the surface in order to alter landscape experience. This landscape experience becomes the design of the surface, as the visual element is not a reflection of the landscape, but an interpretation of information.

Identification of Idea stems from the process of unpacking matter, where simulation is generative and speculative. Through visually recreating an existing condition, this unpacked and translated matter is used to anticipate conditions which aid design. PEG Office uses simulation as a generative and speculative process through digital mapping to better understand the existing conditions they aim to alter: 'this can enable designers to expand beyond our profession's overreliance on illustrating change – rather than working with it ... Variability and change are built into the thinking behind simulations, and reflect the variability inherent to the systems they characterize.' Simulation decodes the landscape by unpacking the layers of information that form landscape conditions. These layers are infinite and our access to them is limited only by the tools we have available to extrapolate information.

Abstraction allows us to test new connections, through the use of tools, in search of undiscovered outcomes. Now, more than ever, the tool can dictate the information and connections made in the landscape. Sha Hwang and Gaia Scagnetti suggest that the tool itself holds agency as 'successful tools alter the DNA of entire populations, through cost, materials, or even cultural attitudes around aesthetics.' The ways in which tools are used is how they alter the landscape, but are limited by the way we approach them. The paper 'Digital Tools of Multiplicity' similarly describes that tools act solely as a mediator – they are generative in that they allow for ideas but do not generate ideas. 'Tools that help us observe and interact with live processes foster the emergence of intuitive forms of engagement with matter and human agency over it.' Digital tools are explored through their capacity to shape the world, and through their influence on data recording and visual representation. Brian Davis considers how tools can enable visual communication by looking at how tools can move beyond reappropriating analogue processes and their subsequent outcomes and 'reveal and construct relations that are otherwise hidden or latent.' But it is the use of the same tools that allow us to extrapolate data, simulate conditions with more accuracy, and even speculate historical and behavioural information. This historical and behavioural information is quite often left out when digitally abstracting information, as most information is from the physical components of the landscape. However, David Mah uses the narrative of the Manhattan's Commissioner's grid, and abstracted hydrologic and topographic information, to unveil latent matter and triggers within the site that enable us to imagine an alternative Manhattan.

Historical information is not limited to speculations or in depth abstraction. Minimaforms seek to create new forms of communication and interaction by bringing behavioural information to life. Projects such as Petting Zoo and Memory Cloud encourage this creation of communication between people, and between people, machines and the landscape. Usue Ruiz-Arana's installation adds behavioural matter into the landscape, allowing us to engage with a 'mundane city,' and to explore how adding a non-physical component into the landscape can alter the way it is approached and perceived. The installation gives way to a new translation of space that exists beyond just the surface. It allows a response, decoding and translating new layers of communication and interaction.

Transformation and invention are inseparable functions: both are quality producing processes that describe the coherent flow of matter through time and it is time that makes the new both possible and necessary.[2]

Viewed as the infinitely complex relationships existing in a singular location and beyond a 'digital ecology', the nature of Digital Landscapes eludes the processes of categorisation and organisation. Technological advances continue to expand cognitive boundaries and little excuse for simplification remains. Increasing accessibility to the layers of information provides us with a renewed appreciation of the power of abstraction to assist us to attain clarity and purpose of outcome.

The ground as an outcome of ecology is a reflection of our generative approach to the landscape using simulating, fabricating, and augmenting as techniques to decode and translate the landscape and its functions. These processes together form a digital ecology that impacts the way the landscape is approached and altered in the quest to find necessary meaning in new forms of communication and interaction. Digital and landscape are reflections of the infinite ecologies that coexist and surround us. One is often the surface of the screen, and the other is the outcome of the ground: both are the polished surfaces which allow us to catch a glimpse of something we do not always fully understand. The surface of the screen, and the outcome, are never static.

There runs an invisible thread that binds one living being to another for a moment, then unravels, then is stretched again between moving points as it draws new and rapid patterns so that at every second the unhappy city contains a happy city unaware of its own existence.[3]

The alterations to the digital landscape are the ways in which we attempt to decode and translate matter and information that is permanently connecting and interacting with the components of the landscape. Through exploring digital landscapes we can derive a better understanding of the ecologies that shape the world. That understanding can assist our search for insights into how we can dictate change.

1. Gilles Deleuze, 1987. A Thousand Plateaus: Capitalism and Schizophrenia. 1st Edition. University of Minnesota Press.

2. Sandford Kwinter, 2002. Architectures of Time: Toward a Theory of the Event in Modernist Culture. Reprint Edition. The MIT Press.

3. Italo Calvino, 1978. Invisible Cities. Edition. Harcourt Brace Jovanovich.

ECOL

DIGITALOGIES

THE LANDSCAPE IS A SELF REGULATORY SYSTEM THAT IS NEVER STATIC. THE MATTER THAT MAKES UP ITS MATERIALS CONNECT, INTERACT, AND COMMUNICATE THROUGHOUT IT. THE EVOLUTION BETWEEN THE PHYSICAL AND THE DIGITAL DRIVE THE LANDSCAPE'S BEHAVIOUR AS MATTER FORMS AND REFORMS.

After modify: on models and other realms

Bradley Cantrell
Justine Holzman

Perhaps all boundaries are illusory, whether erected by ourselves through our lack of information about the nature of things, or by the choice of an oversimplified (or even overcomplicated) model of reality?

John D. Barrow[1]

During the past two decades the separation of the 'digital' and the 'analog' has become increasingly less clear but semantically we choose to continually differentiate these spaces. The 'Digital Landscape' is a construct that fulfills our need to differentiate between the processes of the physical world and the processes of virtualisation. While these realms have functioned within two conceptual spaces, this form of differentiation between analog and digital, or physical and virtual, is collapsing. This perceptual collapse is predicated on the complexity of interactions between analog and digital realms described by the continual overlap of physical entities and computational models. These models are carefully crafted from continuously collected data through sensors, inputs, and interactions, in which acts of sensing and monitoring engender landscapes of 'translation', a form of 'decoding' or 'knowing' that become acts of modification.

The contemporary landscape, is a product of anthropogenic influences intricately enmeshed and shaped by the digital. The landscape, as a territory of operations and negotiations between material and computational logics is more appropriately observed through devices that extend our senses. The perception of the physical world by human senses, replicated through sensory technologies create abstractions inherent to devices, machines, and synthetic organisms. The feedback loop comprised of extended human senses, the representation of the landscape as model, and the subsequent modifications of the landscape irreversibly stitch together the physical and the digital. Model making, derived from the sensing and translation of data as an integral part of the feedback loop between human intent and the physical landscape promotes itself as an actor in the modification of the built environment.

Landscape architecture has developed a dialog that privileges a form of authenticity exuding from the dirt, plants, and physical materials of the profession. While there is an underlying truth to this experience, we are being confronted with a new reality, one that hinges upon a landscape enmeshed in digital and analog spaces. What has evolved is an alternate space, accessible through databases and simulations, that create the justification and capability to assess landscape conditions and proposed goals. The 'digital' or 'virtual' space is active, created for specific applications and evolved through successive iterations. The 'digital' is a pervasive space, shaping the physical world while receiving feedback and evolving through these interactions. The entwinement is deep enough to render the term 'digital' obsolete; to be uttered when speaking about the discrete data stored as 1s and 0s, not the complex forms of virtualisation that are managing,

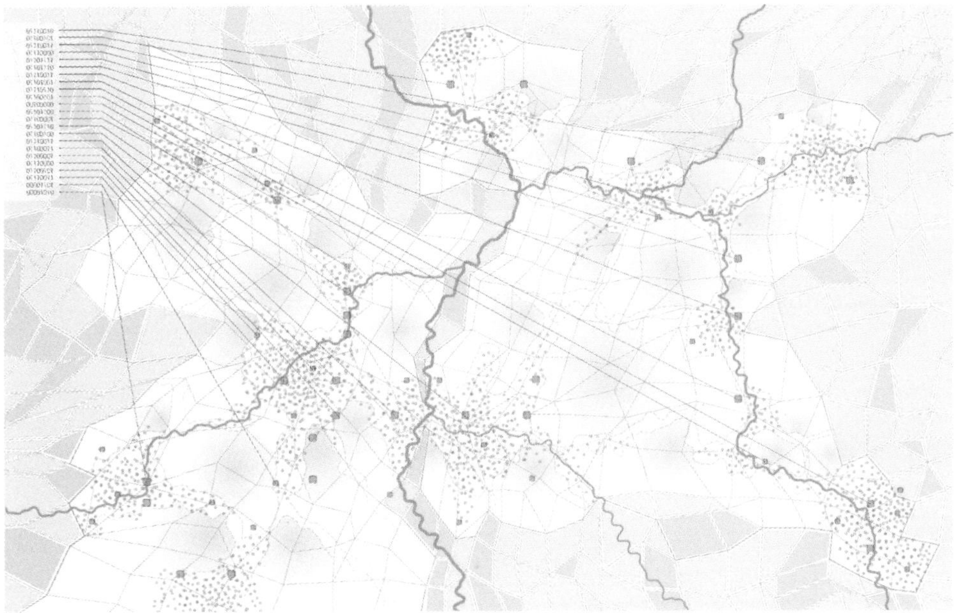

Responsive Landscapes
Susan Cantrell

modifying, and codifying our relationship between devices and organisms.

These complex forms of virtualisation are hybrids — designed to interface with synthetic landscape logics evolving in parallel with biotic systems. These hybrids are composed of models, sensors, instruments and devices all working in tandem to render our physical and virtual realms. Most landscape virtualisations fall into a category of computational modelling that describes the morphology of a landscape surface — the representation of a topography utilised to simulate or render infinite narratives. This form of modelling, representation and mapping is the foundational media for describing landscape design proposals. What we see is a tradition of analog representation simulated and reappropriated with digital tools.

Recent installations by artists and designers working collaboratively (and often interdisciplinarily), with accessible technologies in the fields of interactive design and responsive architecture, are beginning to bridge large-scale speculative design proposals. As a bridge, it establishes methods for the application of real-time technologies to address adaptive and non-deterministic landscape strategies. The space of responsive landscapes[2] is emerging through a series of strategies and an array of case studies that begin to illustrate the potential for responsive technologies to bridge digital and physical landscapes. Expanding upon concepts within the field of responsive architecture, where the application of responsive technologies within the built environment presents the opportunity to mediate spatial conditions, responsive landscapes pose larger questions concerning how the growing integration of technology within the landscape alters and provides opportunities for how we perceive, interact and modify the landscape.

Responsive landscapes pose a series of methodologies: elucidate, compress, displace, connect and ambient which build up to modify. Elucidate is the foundation of responsive environments, in which sensed landscape phenomena are rendered in situ to reveal imperceptible conditions and relations. Compress describes the compression and alteration of recorded phenomena over time, to recompose behaviours and processes into human timescales. Displace is the removal and reconfiguration of information to new contexts, virtual or physical. And connect establishes obvious connections for human interactions with the responsive system.

These methods are all interrelated to approach the application of responsive technologies as a method of 'inquiry' into the contemporary landscape as a site of emergent and novel conditions[3]. Rather than assume there is a particular question for the condition of the contemporary landscape, these methods attempt to harness the potential for the translation of real-time landscape phenomena by technological devices to offer an evolving epistemology in ecological systems — one that is deeply embedded within the complexity of ecological interactions existing across physical and digital space. All of these strategies become tools for modifying the landscape, in which the responsive system is designed to shape and alter the physical landscape.

Our cultural artifacts are already the products of technological intervention whether we choose to fully embrace the hybrid, dive into the virtual, or resist the seduction of data. Agricultural landscapes are a significant example hybridising technological interventions and operations with biological material, shaping a significant portion of the terrestrial biosphere. These logics appear through the application of mechanised tools, the redistribution of water resources, the establishment of monocultures, the creation of synthetic species or the simulations developed to test architectural scenarios. The relationship between computational space and physical space is singular, before the singularity[4]. Computing does not need to match a biological entity's complexity[5] any more than a virus needs to be as complex as its host: the symbiosis exists without a pure definition of the digital or biological. Landscape cannot be conceived outside of this surrogate space, a space that no longer exists purely in a beige box that we attempt to access through tangible inputs — shifting instead to a dialogue of resistance[6] and symbiosis that attempts to actively propagate modes of interaction and response. This virtual, surrogate, digital realm interacts deeply with the physical through logics of operation and implementation.

The surrogate recursively exhibits evolving logics deeply embedded within the formation of synthetic environments. Actuated by feedback loops and protocols, the surrogate encounters interference and produces resistance while systematically responding to perceived phenomena. As the surrogate terraforms the landscape, we watch through captured imagery. Copies, visualisations, distillations and propaganda populate across immaterial boundaries. Within this complex assemblage of realities, layers of abstractions conceal the authenticity of perceptions and blur intentions.

These acts of modification slowly evolve hybridised landscape logics through the combination of both digital and biological computation. The surrogate is not in search of a solution or answer, but instead attempts to observe and embed. Beyond technology creating the platform for new devices or mechanisms, the behaviours and logics of computation function as entities. Algorithmic behaviours that are driving devices, simulations and models evolve and contain a physical agency. A form of adaptive epistemology is existing as algorithms, constantly evolving in search of small bits of knowledge. This parallel form of knowledge is evolving with humans and the landscapes or environments we occupy.

The algorithms in parallel with humans and landscapes are modifying one another, taking us physically away from the landscape, but also closer to it. Closer, as we uncover hidden processes and develop modes of interaction between biotic and abiotic systems. Potentially further, as we prioritise information and knowledge of specific conditions leading to increasing modes of abstraction. It is a form of 'nature' that relies on synthesis and novel relationships that are increasing in complexity. While at one point humans were the sole creators of algorithmic 'thought', these entities are updating themselves through knowledge acquired from human and environmental history and from sensed environmental phenomena. A digital space is evolving as computational systems, led by humans, parsing the world and manipulating systems with greater amounts of articulation and purpose. Not only do these systems evolve, but they are also evolving forms of biology.

These acts of visualisation, inquiry and modification are the composite of the known and unknown, the intentional

Actant Terrain
Justine Holzman

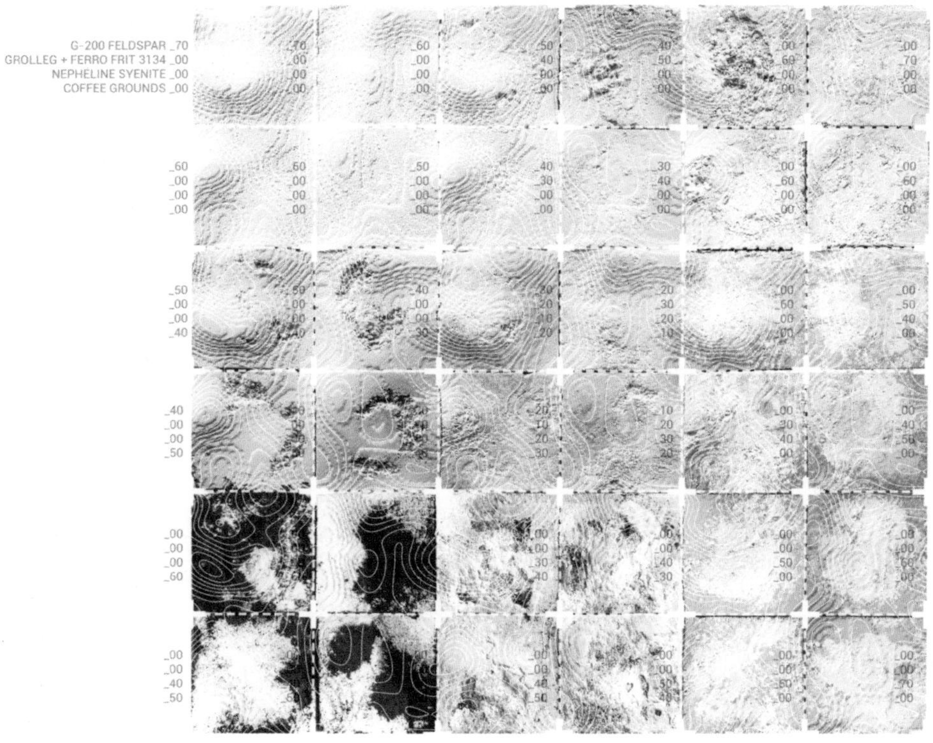

1. Barrow, J., Impossibility: The Limits of Science and the Science of Limits, New York: Oxford University Press, 1999.

2. The field of Responsive Landscapes is described by Responsive Landscapes by the authors is forthcoming by Routledge in 2015. This essay builds upon the theoretical framework outlined by the text.

3. Rabinow, P., Marking Time: On the Anthropology of the Contemporary, Princeton, NJ: Princeton University Press, 2008, p. 3.

4. The technological singularity is the advent of artificial intelligence capable of recursive self-improvement.

5. Makarieva, A., 'Cybernetics,' in Systems Ecology, Vol. 1 of Encyclopedia of Ecology, eds. S. E. Jørgensen and B. Fath, Oxford: Elsevier, 2008, pp. 806-812.

6. Galloway, A. and Thacker, E., 'Protocol, Control, and Networks,' Grey Room, no. 17, 2004, pp. 6-29.

7. Barrow, J., Impossibility: The Limits of Science and the Science of Limits, New York: Oxford University Press, 1999, pp. 22-23.

8. Nechansky, H., 'Elements of a cybernetic epistemology: preprogrammed adaptive systems', Systems Research and Behavioral Science, vol. 26, 2009, pp. 411-427, doi:10.1002/sres.942.

and unintentional — composing realms which deny outright construction, in which there is no outcome — only tuning and nudging, choreographing between and into new states through acts of resistance and ambivalence. The limitations of 'modify' reside in the feedback loop — sensing, processing, visualising, responding and actuating — particularly within the discrete products of responsive technologies. The repercussions are apparent across the contemporary landscape.

The physical evidence of digital computation is revealed across the landscape as permanent marks of organisational space, scars of infrastructural failures and ecological decline, traces of fleeting interventions and clones of repeating landscape typologies. The intentions of these physical manifestations become difficult to trace across the realms of machine and biological intelligence, tangled between the agency and interdependence of digital and biological computation. If instrumentality and feedback extends across these realms, how might we begin to address the physical, virtual, peripheral and intangible territories associated with alien insertions of responsive technologies within the landscape?

In the way that Heisenberg's uncertainty principle and quantum mechanics revealed the paradox of Planck's constant to disprove Newtonian laws of nature with the concept that "even with perfect instruments it is impossible to measure the location and velocity of a body simultaneously[7]", there are limitations to modelling the detailed complexity and expansive interrelations of large-scale anthropogenic and ecological systems. Expanded upon as a metaphor, even if humans were capable of producing an intricately detailed virtualisation of the physical world, the model would never be able to both accurately, depicting one moment in time while mimicking the velocities of individual entities. We are left with the surrogate, a stand-in for which there are infinite hybrids — all far from the comprehensive model capable of complex goal-oriented systems[8] — to partake in small bits, the beginnings of a cybernetic epistemology, whose intelligence relies more on biological interaction than cognitive ability.

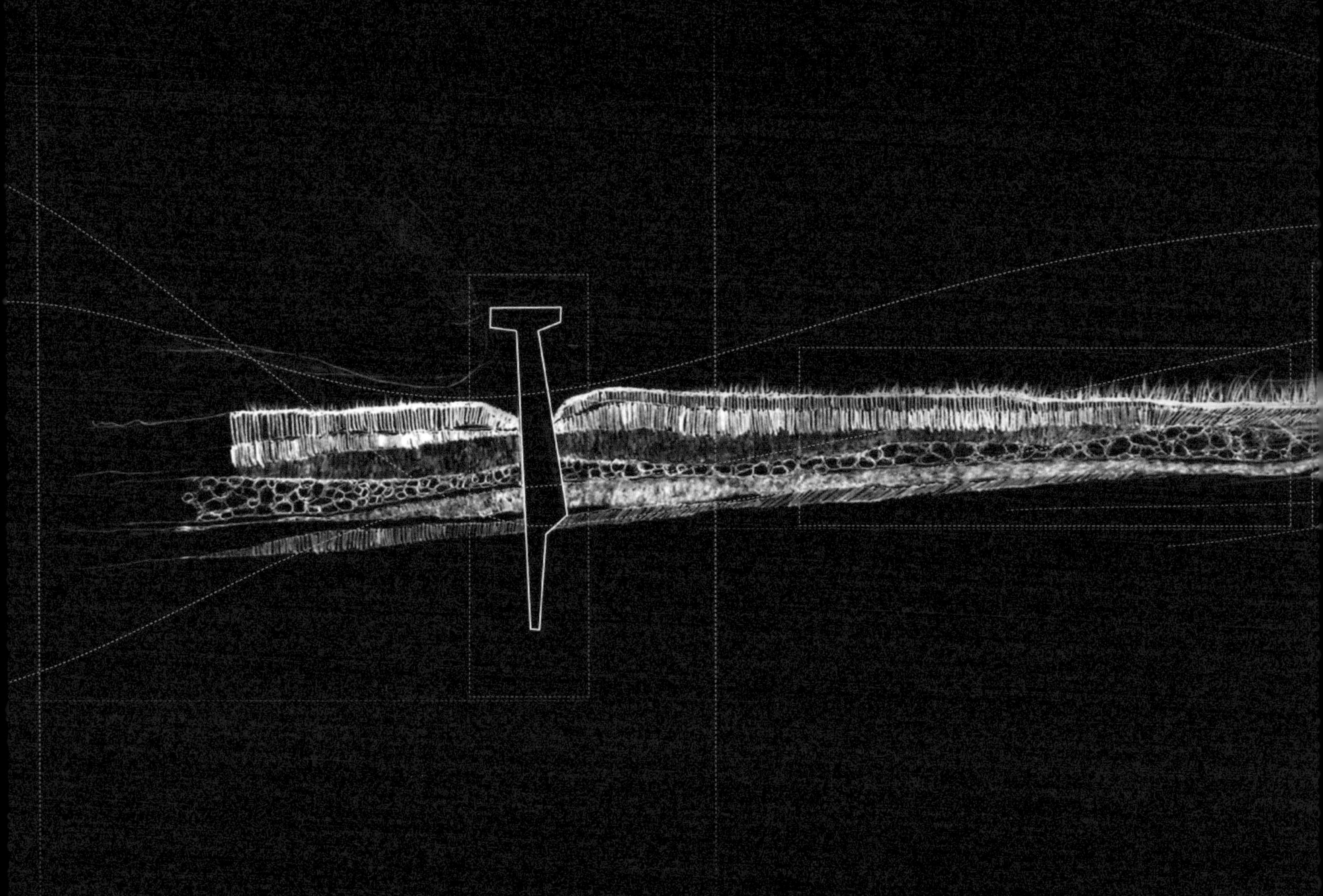

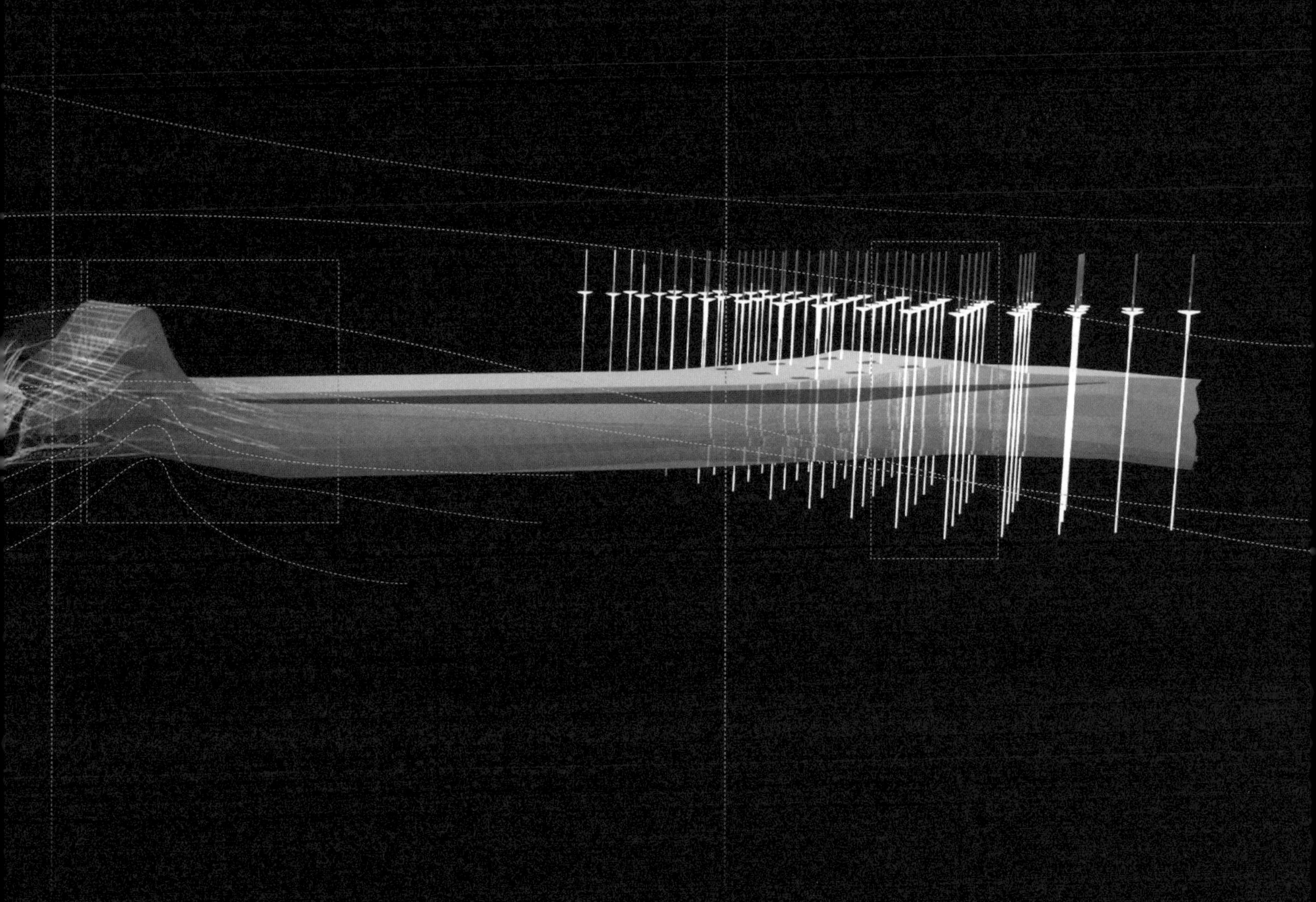

Cyborg Landscapes
Bradley Cantrell, Kristi Cheramie,
Jeff Carney, Matthew Seibert

“The Majesty of Desolation”: Ryoji Ikeda’s digital sublime

Joe WT Scott

JMW Turner
Snow Storm – Steam-Boat off a Harbour's Mouth exhibited 1842
Oil paint on canvas
support: 914 x 1219 mm
frame: 1233 x 1535 x 145 mm
painting
Tate. Accepted by the nation as part of the Turner Bequest 1856

The limitlessness once found in nature gives way, in technology, to a limitlessness produced out of an idea which is not interested in being an idea of nature, but one which replaces the idea of nature.

Jeremy Gilbert Rolfe[1]

In 2013, Japanese-born Paris-based artist Ryoji Ikeda exhibits Test Pattern (No.5) at Sydney's Carriageworks. The warehouse-like interior is recast with a tapestry of binary information. These are not randomised projections, but rather reams of digital data, the kind of information increasingly invisible to us, given a fleeting physical form. Audible modulations effect an even greater disorientation, a speckled staccato static of foreign knowledge. Undulating lines of data spread through the space with an immersive, monochromatic liquidity, enveloping both architecture and audience. The rapidity of the projection creates a zoetrope of disorientation, like a scene from the window of a speeding car, a subterranean nightclub, a haywire LCD screen.

In this precarious impermanence, there are stark and confronting referents to the objective world. In all its digital form, this is a site of mountains, oceans, canyons and torrents, collapsing and rising again into skyscrapers, stock exchanges and global cityscapes. It is impossible to retreat to the edges of the scene, to gain a critical stance or point of reference. The subject is enveloped in a moment outside of time, too much in the spasms of its immediacy to comprehend broader ramifications. There is a deeply captivating, yet fundamentally unsettling, sensation at work. This is the digital landscape.

Here, Ikeda offers a digital ontology, transmuting the data that silently thunders through our laptops, smartphones and internet connections into audiovisual projections, soundscapes and performances. While the digital world is increasingly governed by big data, the "digital sensors, computer networks, data storage, cluster computing systems and cloud computing facilities", these flows of information are becoming increasingly covert, ever more invisible[2]. As Donna Harraway contends, "Our best machines are made of sunshine; they are all light and clean because they are nothing but signals, electromagnetic waves, a section of a spectrum."[3]

In Ikeda's shift from clandestine to clarity, the artist mounts a challenge to the most fundamental dualisms that act as the axes to our digital topography. Nature and technology. Object and subject. Immediacy and duration. Surface and depth. Naturalisation and aberration. Pleasure and terror. It is this collision, the challenge to comprehend the magnitude and immenseness of the digital, that places Ikeda in the lineage of the Sublime.

In Critique of Judgement, Immanuel Kant states that the Sublime is "an object (of nature) the presentation of which determines the mind to think of nature's inability to attain to an exhibition of ideas."[4] In one sense, this notion stems from a material object, that which is "absolutely large ... large beyond all comparison," citing the Egyptian pyramids or the ranges of Mont Blanc as examples. Yet rather than merely monolithic spectacle, Kantian Sublime is an affective and ideological state experienced by the witness. As Eugénie Shinkle considers, "... the sublime object or situation exceeded the limits of the understanding and sensibility; as such, it was not sensible forms or 'things of nature' in themselves which were the source of sublime affect, but the sensation of the failure of the imagination to grasp such things in their entirety."[5] Scenes of great exterior magnitude give way to even greater internal cataclysm for the witness of the Sublime.

The Sublime has historically immerged in moments of anxiety, when global borders are radically shifting. J.M. Turner's painting typifies this attempted exorcism of social uncertainty stemming from a profoundly altering social landscape. Steam Boat off a Harbour's Mouth (1842) and The Great Western Railway (1844) exemplify Turner's typically frenetic expulsion of painterly effect taking aim at the rapid industrialisation of the British landscape and the fundamental re-envisioning of its economy. The protagonists of Tuner's works reside within a dematerialised landscape, utterly dwarfed by object and affect.

Such moments illuminate the impossibility for the individual to comprehend the totality; the disjuncture between reason (finite) and imagination (infinite). From this resulting annexation from the logic of the totality, "Kant's philosophical project" considers Ksenia Fedorova, "was to establish the autonomy of the human subject and its abilities, to distinguish it from the overpowering world of nature"; a moment where "one can be aware of oneself as independent of that which is infinite or ungraspable."[6]

The Kantian model of the Sublime offers a lens through which to examine the immergence of the digital, big data and internet 2.0. It may provide us with accounts of the way in which the digitisation of society and culture has impacted on our collective consciousness. It informs attempts such as Ikeda's to visualise systems residing at the limits of our current comprehension in their scale, velocity and ideological ramifications,

1. Gilbert-Rolfe, Jeremy, Beauty and the Contemporary Sublime. Allworth Press, New York,1999.

2. Bryant, Randal E., Katz, Randy H., Lazowska, Edward D. Big-Data Computing: Creating revolutionary breakthroughs in commerce, science, and society. www.cra.org/ccc/files/docs/init/Big_Data.pdf.

3. Haraway, Donna. "A Cyborg Manifesto: Science, Technology and Social Feminism in the Late Twentieth Century." In, Simians, Cyborgs and Women: The Reinvention of Nature (New York; Routledge). 1991, pp. 149-181.

4. Kant, Immanuel, The Critique of Judgment. Hackett Publishing Company, Indianapolis. Ed 1987.

5. ibid. p. 232.

6. Fedorova, Ksenia. New Media Art and the Technological Sublime. Acta Academiae Artium Vilnensis. 2012, Issue 67, p. 33-44.

7. Hermanson, Robert D. The Contemporary Sublime: Liminal Oscillations. http://www.acsforum.org/symposium2011/papers/hermanson.pdf

8. ibid, p.3.

9. McCosker, Anthony and Wilken, Rowan. 2014. 'Rethinking "Big Data" as Visual Knowledge: The Sublime and the Diagrammatic in Data Visualisation', Visual Studies, 29.2: pp.155-164.

10. Ruskin, John. Modern Painters, Volume IV. Smith, Elder, and Company, 1856. p.361.
11. Eugénie Shinkle. Video Games and the Technological Sublime. Tate Papers Issue 14
http://www.tate.org.uk/research/publications/tate-papers/video-games-and-technological-sublime

"While the screen itself is finite its information is open-ended and thus infinite, harbouring both the potential for pleasure as well as pain."[7] Robert D. Hermanson notes the paradox in the fact that while our screen-based culture grows increasingly omnipotent, there is impossibility of representing and thusly knowing such terrain[8]. It is this amalgam that generates ambiguity. "Data visualization lies at the heart of this ambivalence, offering on the one hand broad, untrained and immediate access to the knowledge assumed to be contained in big data, but also the ability to test its representation capacity."[9] McKosker and Wilkin locate the nexus of the mathematical sublime in big data. Imagination (visual representation) interacts with reason (invisible data) to produce the affective capacity that lies at the present limits of understanding.

Tracing the trajectory of the sublime to its present-day iterations informs the discussions of the way in which technology continues to be asserted as a naturalised, organic state. Ikeda reminds us of the present unknowable nature of the digital landscape, the fluidity and flexibility of its trajectory and the resolute capacity of its user base to collectively shape its interpretation. Sites such as Ikeda's do not seek to naturalise the digital, but rather to give its topography form. An impermanent and oscillating mapping ambivalently extends, yet simultaneously reverses, the logic of the digital landscape. Its encroaching invisibility is made precariously and momentarily visible.

The visualisation of the ever-increasing digitisation of our surroundings, and the resulting mobilisation of affect and ideology, is key to expanding the limits of our understanding of its implications. Ikeda's sites demand a focused attention to these engagements in the re-emergence of an exploratory criticality of the digital landscape. The more the digital landscape becomes reduced to beautified surface, the more it becomes invisible, unquestioned and normalised. It is not the digital itself, but rather the way in which we conceive of the digital, which is problematic. It is the act of sustaining, not erasing, the tensions between imagination and reason invoked by the Sublime which may produce places of purchase and modes of investigation.

The "majesty of desolation" John Ruskin saw in Turner's landscapes may no longer be as corporeal, as overwhelmingly tangible.[10] It is now ever more affective, less objective. Less on the peripheries of our reach and more the fabric of everyday life. More unstable, less overwrought. Brushstrokes have given way to light signals, mountains crumble to data. "Anxiety and boredom, elevated emotion and banality" are the governing forces of the Digital Sublime, the result of the collision between radical possibility and ideological ambiguity.[11] As if in a dream, we increasingly find ourselves citizens of a landscape that remains radically unknowable to us. Yet to question the supposed organic nature of this space, to interrogate and give form to its terrain, is to offer a glimpse of its rules and laws and suggest a momentary foothold for critical reflection.

Multiplicity of landscape arrays

Thomas Mical

Economic necessity forces innovation and introspection. Now is the time to open up new investigations of soft replacements for the formal devices of landscape ordering systems of the past. The twenty-first century exemplary designs should grow from wider discussion of new geometries, new formations, and new organisational protocols in an era of computation and alterity. The landscape, as concept and device, goes soft when the parameters are removed from literal site inscription and imbedded into site thinking/site analysis. This presumes a search for landscape formation procedures that arise from — not simply represent — arrays or loops or other procedural geometries, but that can also sample elements from diverse cultures and contests, to introduce alterity and otherness (noise) into design development (signal). This fusion can structure the designer's imagination to scan and search for new models of dynamism and, more importantly, new models of exchange between chance and control in the formation of landscapes, broadly defined (and defined procedurally).

Landscape is in flux, but even this flux can be determined and designed. Landscape protocols have always referenced the transitive, changeable, cyclic, and punctuated equilibrium dynamics of natural processes, and it should be possible to place this dynamic model at the centre of the field, so to speak, in landscape analysis for landscape design. The resultant soft landscape conditions would pair alterity and difference into topologically formed (or deformed) or interrupted field conditions, perhaps as spaces mapped as subtle changes of state over time, and involve the designed emergence of transient territories, including differentiated micro-conditions.

Urban landscapes, rural landscapes and ideal landscapes belong to an intellectual tradition of the concept of framed and mediated nature, of artifice. Artifice is becoming synthesis, requiring analysis of the formative devices (literal and metaphoric) that form landscapes. Design here is the design of higher-order systems that allows diverse fluctuations in the human activities and the spatial knowledge of machined natural systems. The mutable and transient conditions as the location of identity and meaning in a

Each landscape is, in fact, a multiplicity of landscapes (through use or perception), and this potentiality of multiplicity is the communion between computation and alterity.

landscape, contra the distinct boundary conditions and formal devices used to contain and constrain nature. The Hegelian separation of mind reflecting separated nature can be rethought in terms of forms of growth of eclogues of ideas, requiring us to expand the notion of landscape to include new (animated) diagrams, notations, and vocabularies for examining the formless, informal, and fugitive qualities of physical states of being. Each landscape is, in fact, a multiplicity of landscapes (through use or perception), and this potentiality of multiplicity is the communion between computation and alterity. Rethinking this communion as a landscape design protocol, in light of the possibilities of new practices and procedures, we can identify two related influences: (1) the computational impulse, from data-mapping and remote sensing, to procedural operations for landscape genesis and landscape transformation; and (2) the era of alterity, social and cultural difference and deformation, as it is manifest in the spatial and construction logic of landscape operations. This new integrative theory of landscape, between computation and alterity, is proposed as the engine of innovation, inclusion, and transformation.

"Alterity is disruption and thus it involves a distancing and a positioning that is necessarily apart from the homological relation between form and function[1]." The metrics of determinist space are for control. Within interwar modern architectural thought, the imminence of materialist space frequently functioned as continuum, medium or void. In the modern, claims for a universal modernist spatial logic of instrumentalised event-spaces almost accomplishes the goal of a purely rational distribution of events within a transparent homogenous spatial field. The concept of an unchanging uniformity of space is an obstacle. Significantly, Henri Lefebvre's critique of this modern spatial logic in his influential The Production of Space (1974) necessarily utilised difference, specifically the distinction between conceived, perceived and lived spaces, as analytical tools. Lefebvre states:

"... the aim is to discover or construct a theoretical unity between 'fields' which are apprehended separately ... The fields we are concerned with are, first, the physical —nature, the Cosmos; secondly, the mental, including logical and formal abstractions; and, thirdly, the social. In other words, we are concerned with logico-epistemelogical space, the space of social practice, the space occupied by sensory phenomena, including products of the imagination such as projects and projections, symbols and utopias[2]."

This multiplication of difference is also the tool for design of multiplicity and alterity, which could lead to the necessary emergence of the irrational, the formless and the unknown others into rational control space. Imagine a new taxonomy of landscape spaces becoming-soluble, becoming-indeterminate, or even becoming-fugitive, where the rationalist logic of modern space, surrenders a distinct identity over time in favour of processes of dislocation, disappearance and perhaps the contingency of radical change.

Let us consider that a designed landscape is not a field but an array, as a potential. It is logically (and topologically) beneficial to identify the range of possible (and impossible) landscape arrays for a given location, to open that landscape up to generative (or disruptive) operations and procedures to widen the range of possible landscapes (this would be the definition of the reservoir of landscape multiplicity). It is of extreme interest to look to the boundary of the set of possible landscapes, and how this set brushes against the set of impossible landscapes, for in that seam the highest probability of alterity can be logically located. The formation of possible and impossible landscapes, as procedures, requires establishing higher-order landscape formative geometries and procedures: ones that would follow unusual decision trees and other sorting logic, from genetic design and informal algorithms, to arrive at a great range of possible solutions and configurations, invested in mutability and impermanence. These hypothetical design processes and procedures are process language about unfamiliar possibilities and potentialities — in some cases verging on the impossible, as the upper limit of the landscape imagination.

The final innovation born of this period of introspection is the necessity of something like an aesthetic of landscape-events. Something to replace fixed optical judgement of landscape designs with a more robust model, incorporating human perception and subjectivity into the dynamic model

1. Benjamin, Andrew, Architectural Philosophy, p.41

2. Lefebvre, Henri, The Production of Space, pp. 11-12

3. Deleuze, Gilles, Bergsonism, p. 38

of landscape processes, landscape multiplicity, and potential arrays. The call for soft procedural landscapes is this new model of landscape multiplicity, composed of the porous and soluble quality of experiential spaces in the engineered landscape procedures of the present. To thus animate the notion of landscape generates an emphasis on the alterity, difference and social multiplicity that thoughtful designed landscapes engage. For landscape, as multiplicity, must engage two manners of multiplicity (as split by Deleuze):

"One is represented by space (or rather, if all the nuances are taken into account, by the impure combination of homogeneous time): It is a multiplicity of exteriority, of simultaneity, of juxtaposition, of order, of quantitative differentiation, of difference in degree; it is a numerical multiplicity, discontinuous and actual. The other type of multiplicity appears in pure duration: It is an internal multiplicity of succession, of fusion, of organization, of heterogeneity, of qualitative discrimination, or of difference in kind; it is a virtual and continuous multiplicity that cannot be reduced to numbers[3]."

The fusion of these two types of multiplicity would redefine landscape as a conceptual filed condition, animated by these two types of multiplicity. The soft landscape condition proposed here, in its multiplicity of possible future arrays, becomes a deliberately and permanently unstable mechanism form mobilising fugitive space and sensing alterity.

ARTIST PROFILE : JANET LAURENCE

I am making propositions through works by creating spaces of perception that can bring us into contact with the 'life-world'. Our porous bodies breathe in and spill out into the world. To recognise this interdependence is the ecological undercurrent within my work.

Exploring notions of art, science, imagination, memory, and loss, Janet Laurence's practice examines the interconnection of life forms and ecologies and observes the impact that humans have on the threatened, natural world. Laurence's work addresses our relationship to nature through both site specific and gallery works.

Experimenting with and working in varying mediums, Laurence continues to create immersive environments that navigate the interconnections between all living forms. Her practice has sustained organic qualities and a sense of transience, occupying the liminal zones, or places where art, science, imagination and memory converge.

Top: *In Stance Of Memory (Memory)* 2005
duraclear on shinkolite,
oxides and ash in oil, rusted steel
100 x 600 x 10cm
Collection – Art Gallery of New South Wales,
Sydney, Australia
Photography by Diana Panucci

Bottom: *Rape of the Styx (from Crimes Against the Landscape series)* 2006
duraclear, shinkolite acrylic, mirror, glass,
ash, oil, pigment
60 x 400cm
Collection – Museum Kunstwerk, Eberdingen,

Opposite: *Gold In Green (Landscape and Residues)* 2006
Duraclear, shinkolite acrylic, aluminium, oil, pigment

Below: *The Green That Was (Crimes Against the Landscape) Styx Forest Tasmania* 2009
Duraclear, polished aluminium, pigment on acrylic, mirror, burnt wood
Collection – University of Queensland Museum, Brisbane, Australia
Photography by Patrick Gorman

A Conversation with : ROD BARNETT

The Landscape as a self-regulatory system that is never static as the matter that makes up its materials connects, interacts, and communicates throughout it. The evolution between the physical and the digital drive the landscape's behaviour as matter forms and reforms.

The landscape is a self-regulatory system that is never static. The matter that makes up its materials connect, interact and communicate throughout it. The evolution between the physical and the digital drives the landscape's behaviour as matter forms and reforms. As the landscape is non-static, materials take on behavioural traits of the matters that make them up. What does abstracting materials do to form better understanding of the connection between matter and the landscape?

How do you translate or simulate whole systems without bracketing off components whose role you are unsure of when you are doing the bracketing? If you are abstracting, you are already getting into situations which some would describe as artificial but it could be very useful because it enables you to concentrate or focus on some conditions. However, because landscape is so dependent on forces, what you do starts to become a kind of construct of the examination. The rules that you use for selection or classification actually construct the material or the matter that you're dealing with. When we look at relationships, just very simply between birds and insects or rocks and trees, the tendency would be to focus on the birds, insects, rocks and trees but not in the sense of other actual components those things connect to. So the question becomes, how do you account for what is missing through the abstraction or translation process? Do you do lots of abstractions or lots of classifications that you hope would be inclusive? Where do you start and where do you stop? So to me, that's a question for abstraction. We are interested in matter; how it moves, compacts, its inputs and outputs, all of that is occurring to 'local rules', but we don't know what the rules are.

Kerb:
Perhaps it is attempting to gain some form of balance or understanding of both.

Yeah, you're trying to do stuff that is virtually impossible. Matter, material conditions and generative materials are working under conditions of extreme openness, extraordinary openness. There is evolutionary potential where the evolution of matter is a question of the preservations that act upon it and I think we try to simulate that in landscape architecture and design. We talk about interventions and systems that we think we can somehow reformulate maybe this way or that way and we can do many schematic drawings or schematic productions of future space as we want but you'll never know which future state is going to be selected by the system.

When the preservation occurs or when the disturbance occurs, there's clarification but to me, what's so extraordinary is the catalytic component that is completely open to novelty. Not even the person who's disturbing can foresee what is going to happen, I think that is fantastic landscape architecture, because it gives us something else. It gives us an opportunity to remain involved in system as it evolves to be continually interacting and as a professional, and to me it betokens a new kind of practice of which I know people are really doing now. You know you're working on a project for a very long time and you're not being certain about its results and not pretending to resurrect or represent what the results are going to be. However there are values and ethics associated with it, you can't just do it for fun. It would be nice if you could do it for fun but the kind of systems that landscape architects are continually intervening with are actually pretty profoundly significant systems.

The translation of matter that gives way to understand the behavioural qualities of materials. Thinking of abstraction as a generative process, does the use of digital tools go far enough in the abstraction of speculating potential future landscape behaviours?

OK, well there's digital tools and digital tools. Let's talk about, say, 3D modelling. Do you regard agent-based modelling as a digital tool?

Kerb:
Yes. A technological tool.

OK, so this takes some kind of agent-based modelling, software or programs such as Netlogo which is a really popular one because it's really, really easy to use. It doesn't really require a kind of hermetic programming language in order to use it. So when you are using Netlogo to learn how certain conditions change through time and under certain circumstances, it's the same issue again. Basically you are looking at how the material or the landscape condition adapts to some kind of new condition, and Netlogo as an agent-based program is really interesting because it enables us to watch what's occurring through time, re-program and add information to. Perhaps the potential pathways that the agents can go down or populate might suit a particular design project or a certain theoretical construct. So you're asking, is the digital software area sufficiently up to the game? Because it can't be. Because genuine adaptivity is really difficult to abstract, and even with Netlogo, you can have lots of sliders on the screen and you can adjust them like a kind of graphic or sonic equaliser for all sorts of conditions, but you are just playing around, you're not really able to think you could say what would happen if it flooded. What would happen if this piece of terrain flooded to this height? What would happen if it flooded to that height? What would happen if it flooded in the winter? What would happen if it flooded in the summer? You are looking for some hard data in order to construct some kind of intervention of each condition you are being asked to redesign, and so you are looking at what happens when it floods under a range of conditions but you're never going to be able to actually to model or simulate the extraordinary fine and specific events. You know the world is complicated and that all sorts of things are like a large mobile assemblage, and so if the floods are to X metres in summer then it will dry out etc., but we forgot to model the response with respect to that parking lot or with respect to that village down the road or with respect to the boating community, so on and so forth. Or you know not even the small questions, the big questions that say that an activity is something that is fascinating to model and it is really useful to model, and digital media really encompasses the lot but they're never going get to the point where we can say with certainty about a particular design proposal things like 'a solution'. That's why I say that these design proposals have always had a kind of contingency about them. If you can accept contention on future occurrences that can't be predicted, then I think that's fabulous and it enables the landscape architect to have a kind of competence and authority about a kind of continual role of adjustment, management and redesign and then events unfold, that's where I think we're getting.

What new approaches to the interpretation of material have you seen adopted, in your experience, with this fabrication process that considers and anticipates new behaviours that materials bring to the landscape?

OK, so I think the landscape architectural blogasphere is full of the kind of contemporary or ephemeral 're' 're', 're' from the use of 'go to' urban conditions, to pop-ups, to food trucks, to all this sort of stuff that seems to be generated out of an intense desire to remain fluid, open and to adapt to conditions. So that's exciting too because it goes away from that type of twentieth century infrastructure that is so static, that decays and can never regenerate itself like a cell. And so when we think about elements that organise and self-organise or self-regulate, we're talking about elements that are larger than a single thing, bigger than a seat, bigger than a tree. I don't mean bigger, literally, but actually more connected than a seat, or, taking into account all the connections. In my experience there are an extraordinary amount of proposals that attempt to enact resilience, enact an adaptivity, and so they're moving away from structural formations and into organisational conditions, aggregations and arrangements that don't have key components in them like an ecosystem. They used to think that ecosystems were reformulated by the movements of the largest element in the ecosystem. But now people realise that the key component of an ecosystem can sometimes be something that's quite small, even invisible: microorganisms or fungi, and not the wolf or the bear or the oak tree. So that kind of awareness about the issues of scale and visibility or indiscernibility has really come through in the way people are trying to deal with adapting design. The idea of design itself is changing. I used to design something; now we design process and assemblages. That's again what I really see happening.

Is augmentation of landscape driving us to a deeper understanding of the relationship of the digital to the translated tactile world by the way we experience the landscape?

I think by augmentation you could be meaning something that has a certain capacity that's out there in the world and then true design is a landscape architectural design where you enhance its capacity, really empower it to achieve more than it can at the moment?

Kerb:
Yes.

OK, so yes, to me the whole landscape architecture project is about augmentation. That's what we do and so if we weren't augmenting it – if we tried to create a higher level of complexity or empower the condition to become empowered – if we were trying to do that, then I don't know what we're trying to do. So there are issues about the relationship between humans and non-humans and because there's a sense still, with respect to landscape architecture and design even, when we are trying to augment conditions but we're augmenting them through a sensitivity or subjectivity that is uniquely human and we aren't really taking it to the point of view to the thing that is being augmented. All the things out there in the world which we like to augment are completely different to us. We really need to understand the nature of that indifference. They are withdrawn from us and we need to really understand them.

A prosthesis is an augmentation, for example; an amputee will get an artificial leg – that kind of prosthetic helps them out. It used to be the case that if somebody needed an artificial leg it would be made of plastic and it looked like a leg. These days, you get a really thin sliver of titanium that doesn't look like a leg but its capacity to perform is much greater than the one that mimics the leg. The old kind mimicked the leg but didn't have the power to enhance in its own capacity, or the capacity of the human being to whom it's been strapped, but the new titanium ones are getting there because they've realised they don't need to mimic the conditions they were trying to augment. My earlier point is that you just need to be careful about thinking that you know best for the world. That's put us in a bit of a position right now, so augmentation is a tricky thing. As long as we can understand the powers and capacities of the things we are trying to work with, and really understand what they want to be and not what we want them to be, well then, augmentation is a good thing.

Kerb:
Interesting. So it's like fighting against them and trying to shape them into what we want or what we think is best for us: it's almost a selfish act in that sense.

Well that's what it's come to and what's got us into the fix we're in. We never really considered that the world had its own reasons for being and that other species' role in the world isn't to be there for us.

Kerb:
It's just our obsession with trying to improve things and make things better.

Yes, and even trying to make things better for them. But inevitably it's for us. I mean, all this is political. Issues to do with the invasive species, sea level rise, climate change, are all about how we are augmenting, if you like. It's all about that. It will all result in us trying to make things better for human beings and forgetting that we're one species among how many other billion.

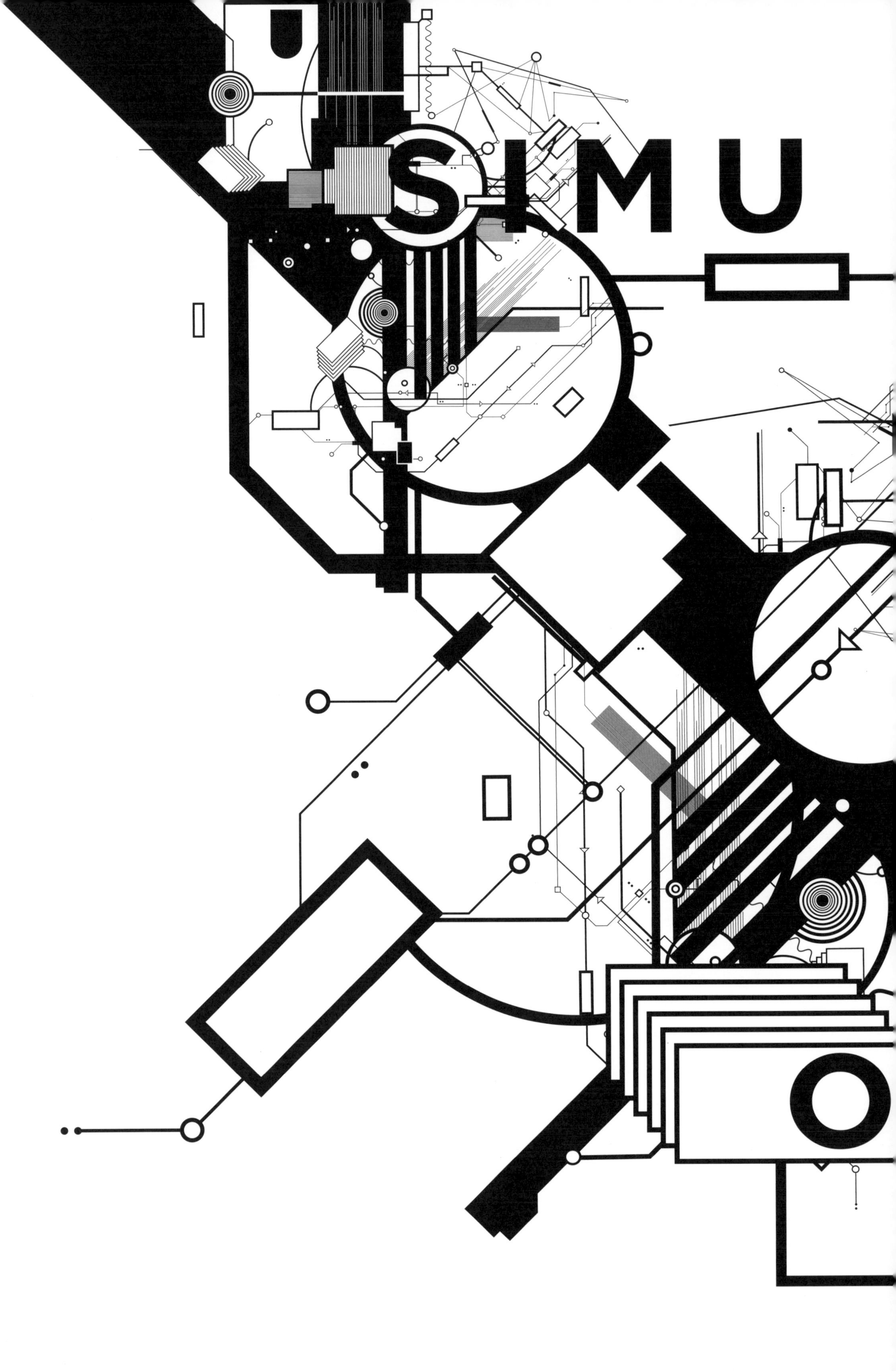
SIMU
O

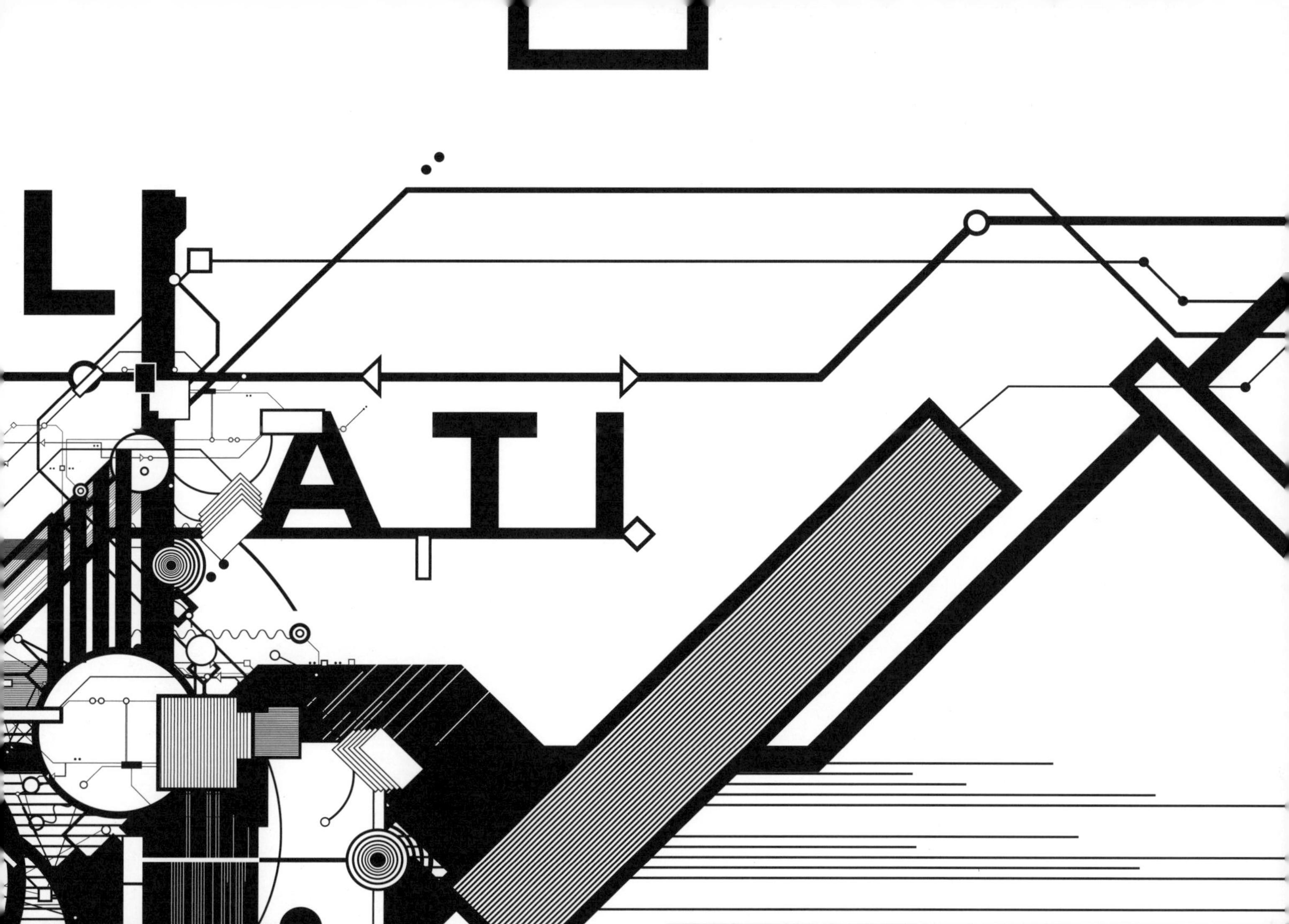

THROUGH THE PROCESS OF TRANSLATING, RECORDING AND INTERPRETING, SIMULATION BECOMES AN ACT OF MODIFICATION. THIS IS WHERE THE PROCESS CEASES TO BE CONSIDERED A LITERAL REPRESENTATION BUT RATHER AN ABSTRACTION. TO BE VIEWED AS GENERATIVE, PROGRESSIVE AND PRODUCTIVE IN NATURE, THE COMPLEXITY OF PHYSICAL ENTITIES DOES NOT NEED TO BE REPLICATED, THIS IS THE PARADOX OF ABSTRACTION.

Project

WATERLICHT

Rosalea Monacella

Designer: Daan Roosegaarde
Date: May, 2015
Location: Netherlands

'Waterlicht' a public space project for the Dutch Water Board. A simulated landscape of waving lines of light evoking the aurora borealis, 'the northern lights'.

Waterlicht is the dream landscape exploring the power and poetry of water. As a virtual flood, it demonstrates how high the water levels might reach and extend into the landscape without human intervention. In this temporary installation people are enabled to experience what the Netherlands might look like without the constructed dyke system, and therefore the effect of the sea again reclaiming the land. The work explores and communicates this through a 1.6 hectare ephemeral landscape in which individuals are immersed beneath flowing lines of light simulating the water flows entering the night's atmosphere.

Waterlicht consists of light made with the latest LED technology, software and lenses. First created for the Dutch Waterboard Rijm & Ijssel, the artwork has occupied Museumplien Amsterdam and has the further ambition to create additional water light landscape that aim to create more awareness of the Dutch water scape.

The innovation is within the DNA of the Dutch landscape via its dikes and creative thinking, that the suggest the Dutch themselves almost seem to have forgotten. Waterlicht is a powerful and poetic experience to remember.

Waterlicht 2015
Lines of light made with the latest LED technology, software and lenses.
Daan Roosegaarde

Landscapes of Math

Brian Davis

The tools of 3D and their capacity to take into calculation memory data, photographs, film combined to a complete geographical, geological and infrastructural data set for any site, indicate a new measure of quality in landscape design. That measure can be called topology.[1]

Christophe Girot

The importance of specificity, the concept of fidelity, the productive tension between precision and looseness, applications of theoretical mathematics, discernment in a data-rich environment: these are some of the most useful and challenging aspects of 'Digital Landscape' representation. In "The Elegance of Topology" Christophe Girot contextualises and explains how they relate to previous representational paradigms such as montage, geographic information systems and perspective. He then goes on to assert that topology — and especially its primary representational form, the point cloud — has the ability to unify the poetic, cognitive aspects of landscape with positivistic, systematic approaches. This potential promises to save landscape practices from the rational, reductive approaches while adding some steel and intellectual rigor to acts of subjective, cognitive, and emotional interpretation. For Girot, the topological model digitally collects and processes data to produce a representation of the landscape that is "local, precise, and culturally specific"[2].

This refreshing argument is picking up steam, and for good reason. It offers the ability to reckon with "the primacy of terrain over an idealized vision"[3]; reality as an alternative to the fundamentally idealised landscapes produced through picturesque imaging techniques such as perspective. And one look at the products coming out of the Landscape Visualization and Modeling Lab — headed in part by Girot at the Swiss Federal Institute of Technology Zurich — is enough to see why this modality is proving so powerful and seductive. Driven in part by technological change, landscape topology critiques the shortcomings of contemporary projects focused on mappings, diagrams, and photomontage while simultaneously furthering similar aims — to get beyond pictorial limitations, to resist positivistic hegemony in description of landscapes (either as systems or places), to deconstruct received notions of value and meaning, and simultaneously reveal and construct relations that are otherwise hidden or latent.

In Girot's topology the way forward is through a focus on continuity. Topology is typically a mathematical term for a type of geometry. It is distinct from the more familiar Euclidean geometry in that it is less concerned with shape and dimension and more with the ability of an object to maintain certain integral characteristics despite constant change. Girot states that when applied to landscapes it has an ability to not only account for geometric coherence of surfaces, but to "integrate heterogeneous fields of action that can be both physical and philosophical, scientific and poetic — integrating past, present, and future potentials into a single meaningful whole. It will bring different design disciplines together to work on a better understanding of landscape as a surface..."[4]. In a concrete sense, this means that the topological model is intended to unify multiple forms of data and representation together within a total digital modesling environment that is simultaneously objective and subjective, precise and interpretive, rational and poetic. While seductive, this focus is partially mistaken.

This concept of landscape topology is undermined by two important but unrecognised conceits. First, it continues the search for a totalising representation — one capable of unifying all other forms of representation. Instead of synthesising through a two-dimensional system where horizontal surfaces can be represented as "great fields upon which real material conditions are isolated, indexed and placed within an assortment of relational structures"[5] as with contemporary mapping projects,

Lidar point cloud of a large bluff in the Lower Elwha River, Washington; image produced by the United State Geological Survey

this version of topology places its faith in three-dimensional digital models. The second underlying conceit is that these models rely on and try to bend all of reality into the theoretical construct of Cartesian space with its implicit assumptions of uniform, limitless extents in all directions.

This was also a fundamental conceit in Corner's mapping project, with its emphasis on milieu as "surrounding, medium, and middle ... having neither beginning nor end, but surrounded by other middles, in a field of connections, relationships, extensions and potentials [sic]"[6]. The local site is then situated in this field condition of potentials, extensions, and relationships that are literally limitless and always in the middle. The intent to unify everything in a model of this type is not only limited, but dangerous. This environment is fundamentally extensive — extending in all directions forever — and relies on the idea that space is a volume that things move around in, rather than something that is produced by the objects themselves. In this model the production of space is not an act of formation, but rather one of colonisation. While this concept of space is useful for conquering societies and designers working for wealthy patrons or with controlled environments (it was primarily developed in fifteenth century Europe, after all), it is a poor stand-in for real landscapes today.

Object-Oriented Modelling

A basic mathematical definition of topology as the study of objects undergoing continuous change becomes radical when applied to landscapes. It is also the least explored part of Girot's formulation, as he is more interested in the linguistic poetic dimensions of topology as applied to landscape. Most contemporary representational projects emphasise means over ends, process over results, relations over objects. These tend to reduce objects to dumb, inert matter that have no inherent capacity for change themselves, but rather await the intentions of some outside agent.

The foundational idea of topology, however, is that objects are in fact capable of change, and yet despite this fact they tend to maintain certain integral characteristics. This refines Girot's emphasis on continuity. Not every characteristic or component is continuous, but some things do persist. Identifying those aspects in a given landscape that are integral to the object and studying how they shift

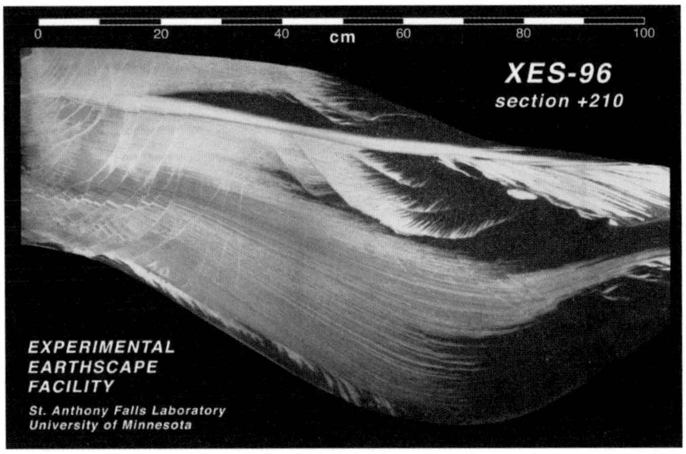

then becomes the key to landscape topology. Girot identifies this[7]. However, it does not then follow that the point cloud is always the appropriate modality for achieving this, but rather it is the ability to monitor, simulate, analyse, and speculate on landscape change using a variety of competing and appropriate methods that becomes critical. And for this, methodologies that focus on change and complexity of landscapes as objects by passing between digital and physical media offer a robust way forward.

While most digital modelling environments are built on the idea of volumetric, abstract, limitless space, physical models are not (some digital models, such as computational fluid dynamics modellers, are not either). Materials are real and have their own limits and capabilities — the universe is not a cube they simply move around in. However, physical models are also slow and hard to make well, and are fairly imprecise, with their fidelity limited by the level of resolution of a routing bit on foam or the roughness of chipboard. Surface modellers, however, are quite strong in these aspects. Using 3D scanners, printers, and CNC milling to pass frequently from one to another rapidly promises the ability to describe and analyse existing conditions and rapidly prototype proposals which are then tested and evaluated according to the values of the project.

Rather than using these capabilities to model in static media, such as plywood and foam, combining them with more dynamic materials allows for more complexity to be undertaken. Experimental sedimentology utilises physical-digital models — highly programmable physical space — a geomorphology table that runs a slurry in controlled ways through a basin filled with specific amounts of modelling particles that simulate the movement of sediments at small scales. The table is equipped with a number of instruments to control flow rates, slope, and to feedback data on the amount and rate of erosion and accumulation. The intent is to try and simulate historical sedimentary processes and thereby test the veracity of place-specific geological theories[8]. Combining this with conventional landscape architectural modelling offers great potential for speculative investigation of landscape dynamics and change over time.

As part of a studio project on the Buffalo River, in New York State, an abstract physical version of a stretch of the river was created in a geomorphology table. A number of simulations were run to tune the processes so that they approximated what was known about the real river. Then, formal speculations were quickly prototyped and modelled on the table. 3D hand-scanners as well as cameras were used to digitally capture the effects of individual runs,

Left:
The Experimental Earthscape System (XES or 'Jurassic Tank') at the University of Minnesota St. Anthony Falls Laboratory can be programmed to reproduce patterns of subsidence, allowing for new experimental insights into the stratigraphic record.

Opposite:
Aerial photograph of a combined sewer overflow event at a public boat dock in Troy, NY; this type of aerial photography is event specific and extremely high resolution though it does have its own limits; part of my 'Visualizing Landscape Change' project, I produced this image with the help of graduate students Petra Marar and Jinhee Ha through my Borderlanda Research Group.

and then a grasshopper definition was used to analyse the resultant meshes for differences in cut and fill. These insights then become a decisive part of a much larger design methodology that folds in conventional forms of representation. In this process it is precisely the conflicts, the aberrant results and the surprises that bring up new and exciting design questions and possibilities.

Reconstructing Topology

Topology is not a philosophical stance that sees everything as continuous, but rather is the study of the ability of objects to maintain a certain characteristic integrity while undergoing processes of constant change. This suggests a few keys needed for the development of a landscape topology. First, practitioners must get out into the field to gain competency in the collection of their own information. We must denature data and understand in a fundamental way that knowledge about a place is an artifact. It resulted from a process. It was produced using instruments (including concepts and physical tools) to understand some aspect of reality and, because of this, all information about a place comes with its own host of built-in limitations and assumptions.

Second, instead of striving to master the new technique, be it the point cloud or parametric model, we must endeavour to become adept at a whole host of representational methods, ranging from the point cloud to the annotated section sketch, to plan and section. Each method is fit for certain purposes and not for others. None of them alone is adequate for undertaking a landscape project, and no single methodology is fit for every conceivable situation. Because of this, it is the discernment in stitching these together to formulate a methodology appropriate to the task at hand that gives value to design judgement, not simply technical proficiency in any one or set of techniques, no matter how sophisticated[9].

Girot's argument does a great service to the first point in one of his most important lines of thinking. It gives new and important emphasis to intentional, considered fieldwork:

Young landscape architects must return to the field, to learn once more how to operate knowledgeably in a landscape. The tendency in recent decades has been to push landscape education towards a higher degree of abstraction and reduction, with an emphasis on communication skills and pattern recognition, rather than on physical design skills ... Consequently, it seems particularly important to return to the concrete physical reality of a site, learning how to identify the character, potential, and inherent qualities of landscape.

These resonant words read as a plea for rediscovering the ability to collect one's own impressions and data, for becoming skilled at simultaneously interpreting embodied experience and operating a quad-copter drone or Topcon® Total Station. As landscape practice has pushed toward higher degrees of abstraction and reduction, and designers learned to stay in the studio and in front of the screen, the data that we mine, download, process and otherwise work with tends to become naturalised. It is no longer understood as an artifact, the result of an historical process, but instead as information that is true or right.

In Girot's landscape, topology data is not only worked with, processed and manipulated, but it must be produced. It is not enough to work with the data produced by other disciplines. But this idea is in need of further development. What intellectual and physical action should be taken to "identify the character, potential, and inherent qualities of landscape"? Let's consider the most ubiquitous form of modern landscape data, the aerial photograph.

1. Christophe Girot, http://girot.arch.ethz.ch/research/design-precision-topology/archives-design-precision-topology/topology-a-new-measure-of-quality-in-landscape-architecture. Accessed 11 June, 2015.

2. Christophe Girot, 'The Elegance of Topology' in Girot, Freytag, Kirchengast, Ricther (eds.), Landscript 3: Topology (Berlin: Jovis, December 2013, 79-115), 82.

3. Girot, 'Topology', 102.

4. Christophe Girot, http://girot.arch.ethz.ch/research/design-precision-topology/archives-design-precision-topology/topology-a-new-measure-of-quality-in-landscape-architecture. Accessed 11 June, 2015.

5. James Corner, 'The Agency of Mapping' in Denis Cosgrove (ed.), Mapping (London: Reaktion Books, 1999, 213-252), 215.

6. Corner, 'The Agency of Mapping', 224.

7. Girot, 'Topology', 104.

8. The Experimental Earthscape System (XES, or "Jurassic Tank") run by Chris Paola at the University of Minnesota at the St. Anthony Falls laboratory in Minneapolis is one of the most compelling and applicable versions of this work.

9. Girot himself begins to acknowledge this on page 95 of 'Topology' when he says that "the plan, section, and perspective are here to stay, but they can no longer precede the renewed understanding of terrain". But it is his adherence to idea that the point cloud-based topological model can unify and smooth over differences, rather than allowing competing approaches, that falls short for now.

10. Clement Valla, 'The Universal Texture', Rhizome, July 31, 2012. http://rhizome.org/editorial/2012/jul/31/universal-texture/. Accessed 11 June, 2015.

11. Evidence of this is presented and dissected in Karen M'Closkey's Structuring Relations: From Montage to Model in Composite Imaging," in Charles Waldheim and Andrea Hansen (eds.), Composite Landscapes: Photomontage and Landscape Architecture (Ostfildern: Hatje/Cantz), 2014.

Aerial imagery mass-produced by large corporations and government agencies has become a pervasive and important tool in contemporary landscape design and urbanism over the last twenty years. This type of data-rich representation offers free and easy to access combined with the ability to study and interpret patterns at very large and very small scales. But this imagery is not true or right. Rather, it is an artifact, the result of a process, with its own limitations and assumptions built in and an inherent ability to teach us. Clement Valla explains how the aerial imagery of Google Earth is mapped onto a 3D model of the globe through the patented system, the universal texture[10].

Google's algorithms select aerial imagery from ever-expanding satellite databases according to a set of rules prioritising daylight images with minimal shadows, no cloud cover, green foliage, and high contrast. That is, the aerial imagery used for landscape design has as much to do with Google's own ideas about the world than with any logic related to a specific place or landscape project. And while these are incredibly powerful and often extremely useful, they may tell us nothing whatsoever about how the landscape appears in autumn, how it functions during a storm event, or how patterns of human use and habitation change throughout the seasons.

Some of these limitations can be overcome with other forms of data – site photographs, recorded oral histories, prior knowledge about the color of autumn foliage of different species in an area. And sometimes this information will be purely complimentary. Other times it will be contradictory, raising a new set of questions that must be investigated or intentionally disregarded. These facts result from "competing inputs, competing data sources and discrepancy in the data". In the words of Valla, they teach us that "the world is not so fluid after all".

This is precisely the point; it is only by intelligently combining multiple ways of knowing and making, testing them against one another and evaluating insights, that a more complex understanding and proposition can be attained. Attempts to synthesise all knowable aspects into a single, seamless representation, especially one built on the conceit of abstract, limitless space (whether two-dimensional as with mapping or three-dimensional as will point cloud modelling) is not only destined to fall short, it fails to leverage the value of design to discern between conflicting information and complex possibilities.

The lure of a single computational environment for revealing and generating alternative landscape futures has never been stronger[11]. And these are truly exciting times, defined by the incredible availability of data combined with the level of abstraction afforded by the computer which allows for high degrees of analysis and synthesis. Many other creative fields have used these developments to make great strides in everything from shipbuilding to architecture to music composition. But landscapes are not architecture, ships, music, or even language. They cannot be so easily controlled, and they cannot be understood as semiotic systems. Rather, they are heterogeneous and unruly objects defined by conflict, competition, change and difference more than seamlessness. A landscape topology that is fundamentally methods-oriented and focused on change, not continuity, is a promising direction for the development of the 'Digital Landscape'.

Digital tools and multiplicity: towards a relational understanding of space, time and value

Eduardo Rico
Enriqueta Llabres
Jung Hyun Woo

The use of simulation of landscape processes, techniques of cartographic representation and digital interfaces can help us move towards a relational form of understanding design at territorial scale. It does so by focusing on how synthetic thinking influences both our perception and definition of time, but also how it addresses novelty within the construction of tacit responses to territorial dynamics. Three projects, where digital tools act as mediator between the designer and the different actors involved in territorial process; this form of openness and multiplicity unveils political tensions behind the design process will be introduced. Synthetic time, as design material, has implications in the political dimension of the territorial project, bringing questions about the nature of the project itself and its form of documentation. The need to understand the political nature behind human agency and its relations to material process can bring further relevance to work with these techniques.

The Projects

The first case, 'Coastal Futures', is an academic project developed in the Masters Landscape Urbanism (Architectural Association). The course researches forms of territorial praxis which work with the intersection between natural processes of formation and patterns of human intervention. The aim is to compile a Pan-European Atlas of radical territories, which challenge conventions of border, ownership and the role of the different institutions across The European Union in shaping our landscapes. The students work simultaneously at geographical and architectural scales in order to generate design guidelines which address what Harvey would call the material processes of social reproduction. Here, the author distinguishes between 'Relational' and 'Socially', given constructions of space and time. In the former, it is possible to have multiple constructions coming from different domains; these domains refer to groups of people that share similar values towards a particular process. Domains might differentiate themselves through gender, disciplinary background or ethnic background. In contrast, socially given constructions of space and time are imposed serving as a mechanism to consolidate material practices of social reproduction, as ways of assigning values by imposition. The academic research, Pan-European Atlas, raises the need to stress a Relational approach to design, where a multiplicity of domains form part of the identity of the European Union and where the specificity of territorial practices are brought to the centre of the design agenda. Here, value is constructed through multiple understandings of a process that cuts across the member countries. The long-term proposal is the possibility of introducing new forms of Pan-European landscape projects as mechanisms of building European values that facilitate institutional renovation across the EU.

'Coastal Futures' aims to build a design agenda that can be inserted within

Figure 1. (Top)
Sediments distribution

Figure 2. (Middle)
Coastal habitats

Figure 3. (Bottom)
Land reclamation and land use

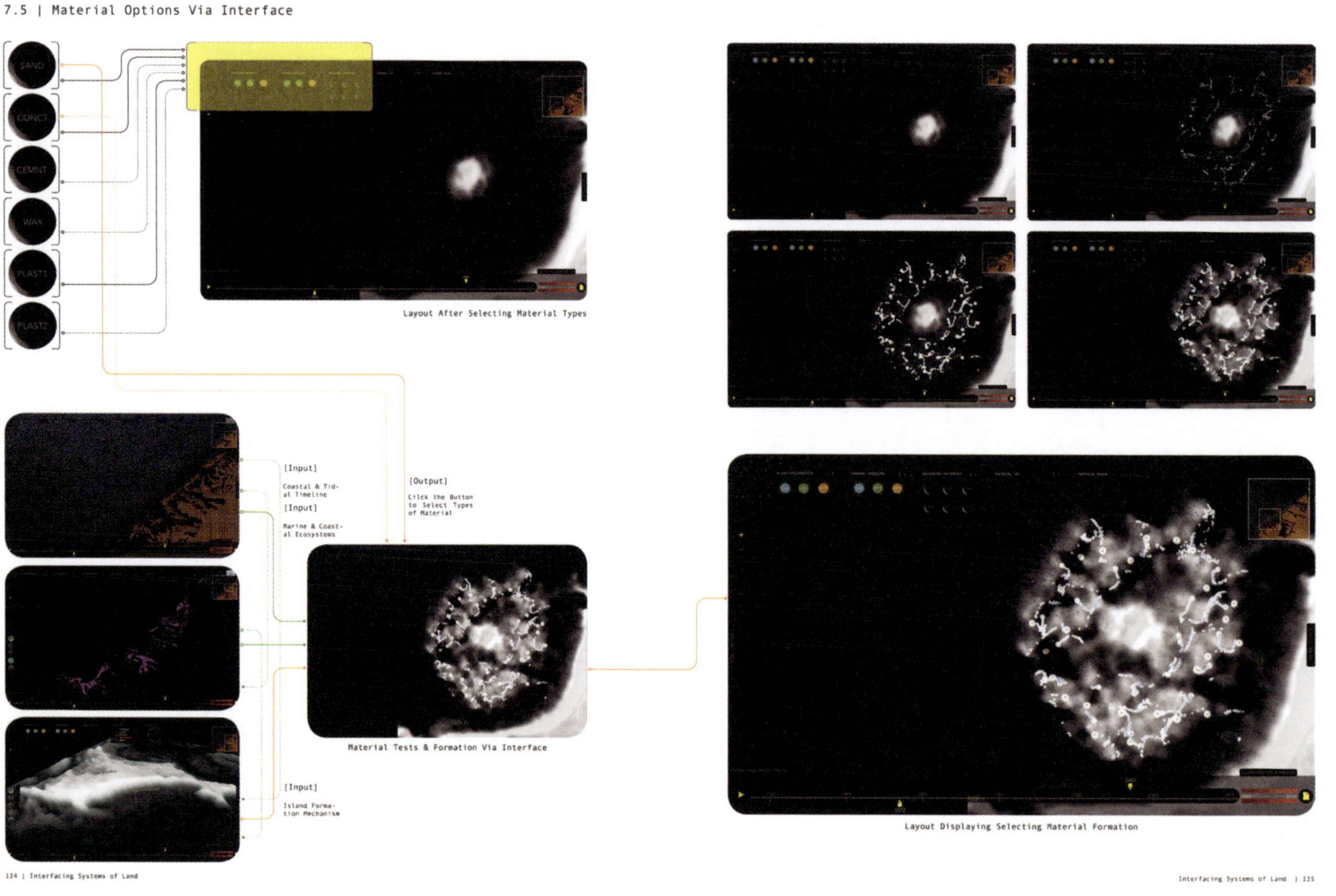

the wider problem of the eroding coastline of the UK. Both sea level rise and geological subsidence in England are increasing the risk of flooding for substantial tracts of low-lying territories on the coast of the British Isles. A common practice in many of these areas is the so called 'managed retreat', where selected pieces of land are allowed to flood in order to generate buffers to help relieve pressure elsewhere and generate new valuable habitats. The project explores how this technique can also be the generator of new forms of economic activities and urban fabric. It does so by looking simultaneously at the small scale of the creek and at the country-wide framework. It explores the mechanisms of controlled erosion and tidal creek generation, given a single inlet-outlet based on a cellular automata simulation model for sediment transport. A number of tests are carried out in order to generate different structures of saltmarshes, according to requirements of different programs which could range from fisheries, oyster farming or ecological areas. This catalogue is then applied in the floodplain beside the English city of Sandwich by studying the intersection of existing land uses and preferential flood routes, generating a landscape of saltmarshes combined with different economic activities around the city. The project attempts to draw attention to the fact that these territorial changes would require new forms of ownership, agreements and spatial solutions in order to share the burdens and benefits brought by the challenges behind climate change. The system is then explored as a blueprint for other areas on the coast, generating an 'Atlas' of the eroding territories of the UK where the dialogue between multiple domains reconfigure the way in which we understand economic and ecologic development.

Figure 4.
Material via relational urban model

While 'Coastal Futures' emphasises the possibility of creating new cultural landscapes affecting its institutional framework, a question still remains as to how the negotiations behind those decisions would take place.

The second project develops a design tool based on an interactive digital interface that orchestrates input and output from digital simulation of geomorphology dynamics, participation and urban policy. 'Interface System of Island in Abu Dhabi Coastline' is an academic project developed within the Urban Morphogenesis Lab (The Bartlett School) which engages with the conflicts emerging from operations of dredging and construction of artificial Islands off the coast of Abu Dhabi (Figures 1, 2 & 3). The proposal departs from an existing interface developed by the local government, The Abu Dhabi Blue Carbon Demonstration Project, which aims to communicate the importance of different ecological habitats by showing its relationship with the carbon stocks of the Abu Dhabi coastline. While this official project stresses the need to understand the ecological value of the different areas of the coastline, it remains mostly informative. The team proposes to add a projective focus to this type of application, with the scripting of an interface that facilitates coastal intervention attending to morphological, economic and environmental logics.

The proposed interface runs a simulation of the process of tidal delta formation within the archipelago along the coast of the Emirate and departs from a landownership pattern based on the environmental service provided by different ecological habitats. The idea is to maintain the overall environmental service within the Abu Dhabi coastline with each of the owners having the responsibility to preserve their own stock of environmental service. In the event that new land uses would compromise the overall environmental service stock, the model allows trade between the different landowners within the coastline so that new land is created to compensate the initial loss. The interface is simultaneously the design instrument, the participatory mechanism and the urban document; facilitating a relational construction of space, time and value while contributing to the spatial qualities that would give identity to the emerging territorial formation.

The use of digital simulation allows the designer to develop a materially-driven design that merges artificial processes of land dredging and island construction with processes derived from tidal dynamics (Figure 4). Time-driven design allows the designer to amplify the sensory information and the development of concepts based on intuitive forms of reading the environmental processes. Here, time-based captures belong to periods of intensity within the design process along the lines of the concept of Duration. Time as duration has to do with the immediate data of individual consciousness; it is immeasurable, intensive and conformed through our perception by distinct sensations that are inseparable from one another. In Bergsonian Time, heterogeneity and continuity coexist within the individual consciousness. It is within time that we can think of multiplicities, bringing us back to the main idea behind the relational construction of space time as defended by Harvey . One could argue that tools that help us observe and interact with live processes foster the emergence of intuitive forms of engagement with matter and human agency over it. If applied at the territorial scale, these tools can ultimately help us think about relational forms of generating the project of the city, where negotiations of different stakeholders take place in a constant interaction with processes of natural emergence. The Abu Dhabi Island Project tries precisely to do this, opening up questions of authorship, public communication and the value of new forms of documentation of the urban project.

The relationship between time and authorship is pushed into the spatial definition of collective values in the third project. In 'Seosomun Park', synthetic time informs the construction of collective consciousness and its relationship with history, bringing the possibility of processual forms of landmarks and icons in the city. Located at a historic site in the heart of Seoul, it

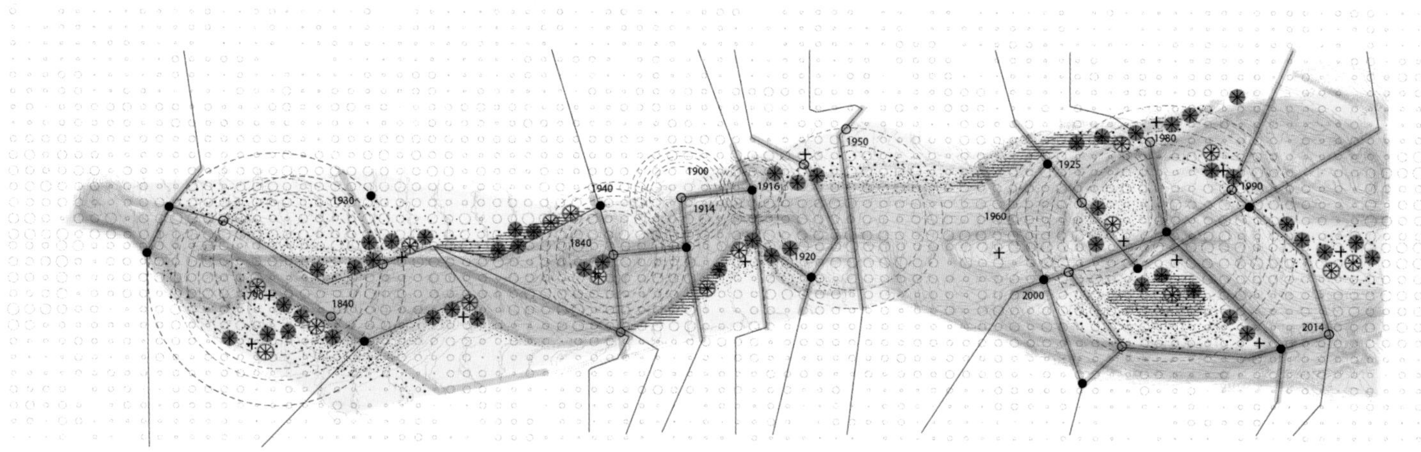

Figure 5.
Proxy model digital capture

provides the status of a landmark with great historical values; as a market, a major gated route into the fortress of the Joseon Dynasty (former Republic of Korea) and a place of pilgrimage for Catholics since 1784. The scope of the project is to build a new church, maintain the destination as a park but integrate it into new planned transportation nodes.

The scale of the church and its relationship with the urban fabric has historically emphasised its position as a landmark, an icon and a place; this historical condition is challenged by the continuous constructions of space, time and value in the existing context. The question is whether time as design material can turn this challenge into projective forms of new meanings. In order to answer this, the project proposes a combination of fixed elements of the landscape, with a form of coded proposal that can evolve over time and is linked to a public design interface.

The project begins with the creation of a landmark by emphasising its underground condition. It excavates the ground, constructing an imaginary archaeology and unveiling historical traces. Two circulation routes are defined. One is dedicated to the religious people and defined by an ambulatory pathway that connects ground with underground (Figure 5). The ambulatory keeps the character of the park but encloses the church into a static condition emphasising its solemnity. In contrast, the west edge of the pedestrian paths enclose a dynamic landscape that is situated in a lower level (Figures 6 & 7). This dynamic landscape is composed of a constantly mutable riparian landscape (redirection of a previously diverted river) a number of fixed components (hard paved embankments) and a number of semi-permanent components (planted edges). The location of the semi-permanent components can be facilitated through an interface that orchestrates a proxy model and a planting scheme (Figure 8). These in turn affect the riparian landscape and, over time, finalise the form of the fixed components. The final aim is to propose a landscape design that continuously builds a relational interpretation of historical layers through landscape performance, unveiling the creation of new meanings.

An immersive position towards the environment is currently overtaking the academic debate within the praxis of digital design; coming from the belief that this will move designers

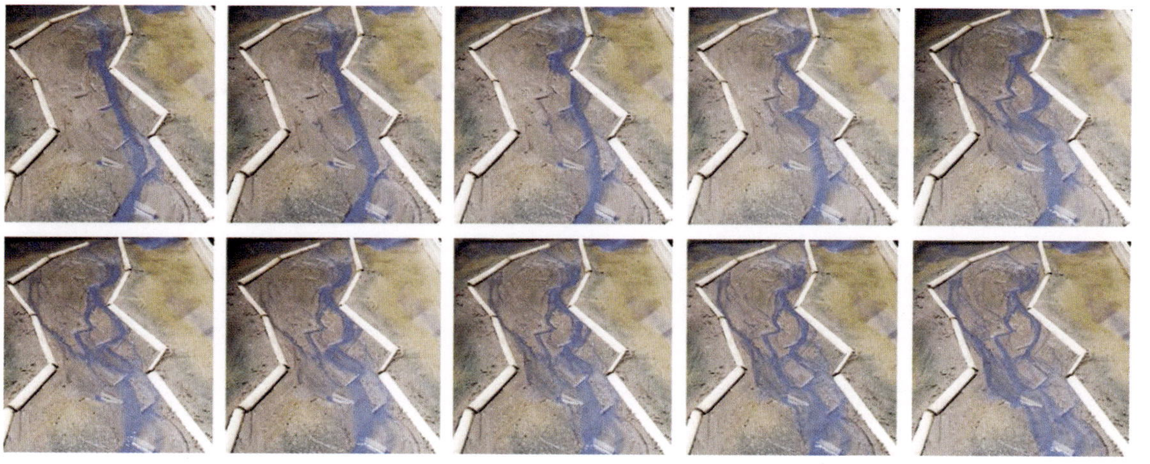

Figure 6.
Proxy model

away from the distant, technocratic and passive approach to 'the Territory' that has been dominant up until the advent of the environmental movement . In this context, and aided by new digital techniques of data capture and simulation, designers have situated themselves in a blurred condition between natural and artificial, rendering the surroundings as "socio natural setting which pre-exists the production of new things" This condition, as Picon points out in his article 'What happened to the Territory' does not prevent us risking a "return to a magical world animated by forces that escape human characterisation". The challenge still remains as to how to unveil and engage with its inherent political tensions.

In conclusion

In the previously described projects, the designer places rules and algorithms (both computational and digital) and design guidelines for others (park users or urban stakeholders) to contribute towards the final result. This idea of shared spatial agency, linked to particular types of documentation, is described by Mario Carpo in his book "The alphabet and the algorithm" . What this article argues is that the engagement with novel forms of documentation and interaction can bring new regimes of authorship, ultimately leading to a relational form of understanding of the design of space, time and value. The challenge would be to maintain a constant awareness of the political and conflictual nature of the decisions behind spatial agency.

A synthetic thinking of time enables humanistic forms of algorithms, bringing back important aspects in creativity such as feelings and intuition. This article advocates that, in the future, digital design practices should move towards tailored design toolkits that act as mediators between the designer and the different actors involved in process of territorial formation. This form of openness and variability will allow unveiling political tensions during the design process facilitating discourses of utopian processes.

Figure 7. (Above)
Church entrance aerial view

Figure 8. (Opposite)
Seosomon park and church
bird's-eye view

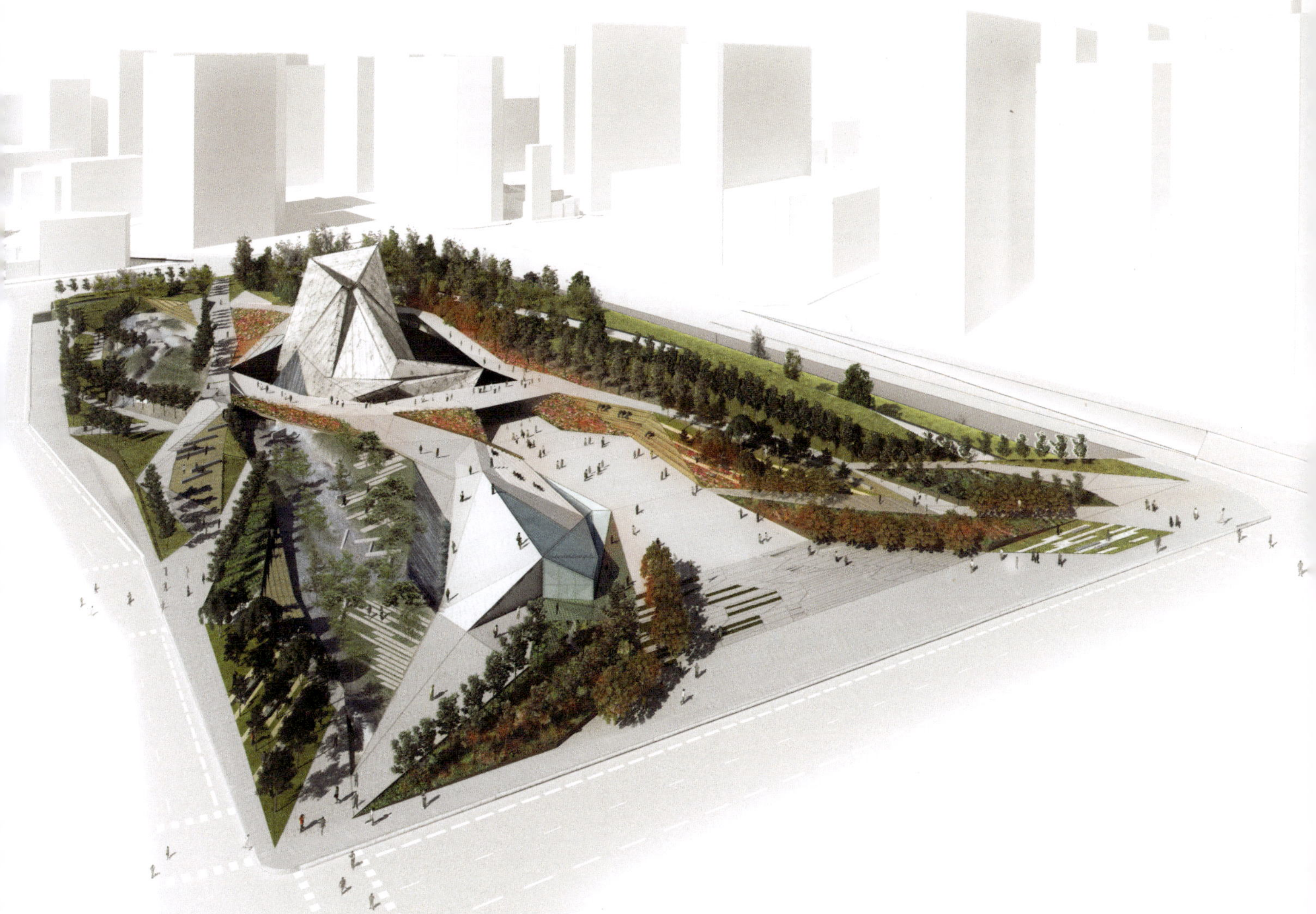

Project

DYNAMIC DELAWARE

PEG Office of Landscape Architecture

Figure 1. (Above)
Tidal wetlands

Figure 2. (Opposite)
Comparison of geospatial data (topography and bathymetry)

Advancements in optical and analytic computation continue to open horizons of insight and understanding about our world. These innovations create new means for designers to engage the temporal and relational qualities inherent to the dynamic medium of landscape. However, landscape architects have been slow to explore the experimental and generative potential of computation; in particular, the simulation of physical processes. Our recent research initiative considers the potential for simulations to expand the landscape imagination in new directions and dimensions.

Philadelphia, like many cities that have shifted to a service economy, is reinventing its waterfronts. A series of recent planning and regulatory initiatives are underway, which aspire to transform the Delaware River from a transportation utility into an ecological and recreational resource (i.e. Green City, Clean Waters; Master Plan for the Central Delaware; Estuary Restoration Act). This transformation will require remaking miles of armoured river edges into 'living shorelines' and manufacturing vast acreages of tidal wetlands (Figure 1). While greening proposals abound within the redesign of shorelines and waterways, two of the most important factors for gauging wetland suitability - energy and elevation data - are typically absent in these re-natured visions. This disregard for the key parameters of living edges has greatly limited landscape architects' abilities to effectively imagine strategies for working with the dynamics of our urban waterways.

Dynamic Delaware, explores wetland suitability strategies that are directly guided by energy and elevation

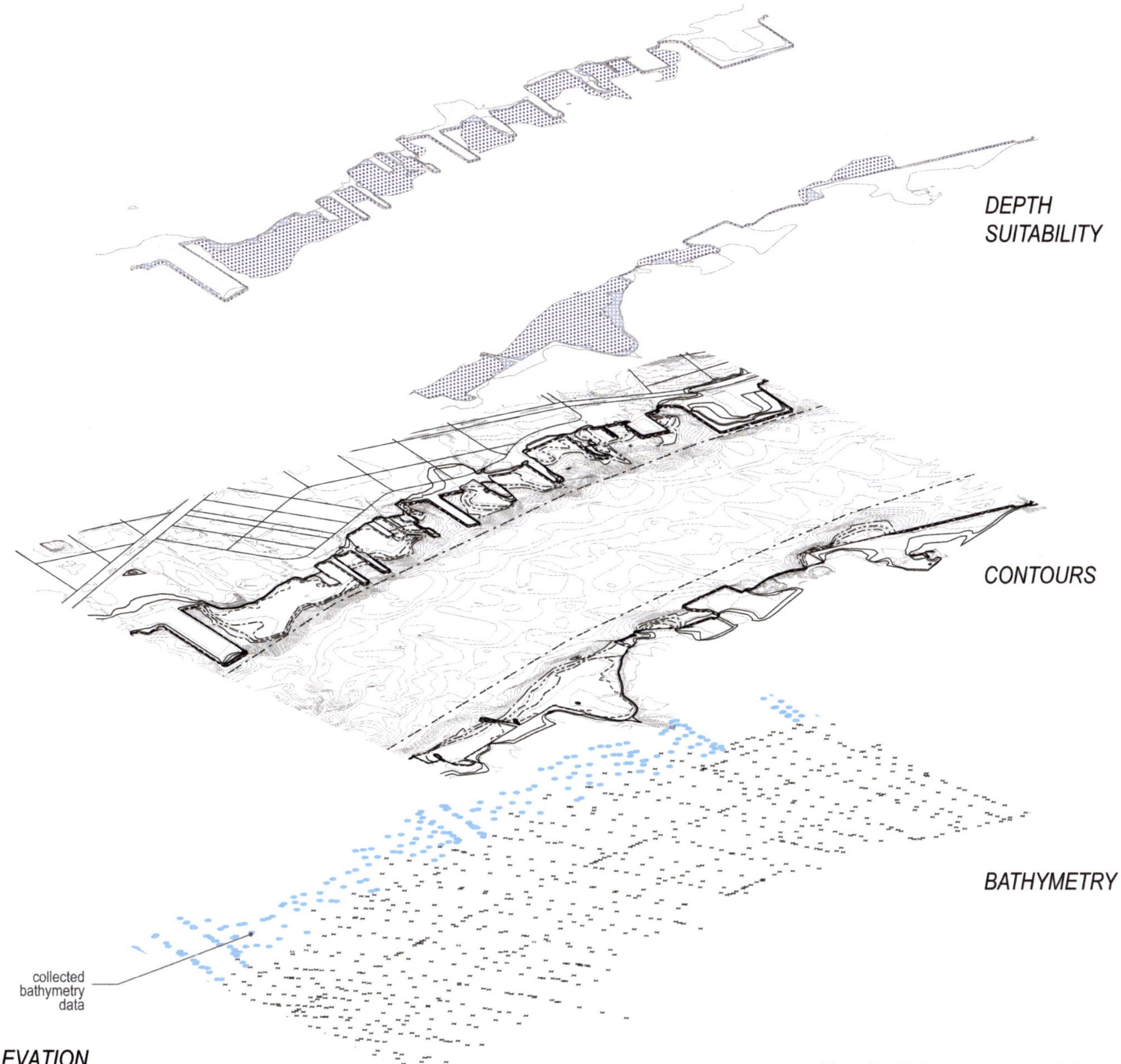

ELEVATION

- *Subtidal Zone*
- *Intertidal Zone*
- *Transgression Zone*

- *1.0 m - 10 y. high*
- *0.1 m - 2 y. high*
- *-0.1 m - MHW*
- *-2.0 m - MLW*
- *-3.0 m*
- *-4.0 m*
- *-5.0 m*
- *Dredging*

Subtidal Zones

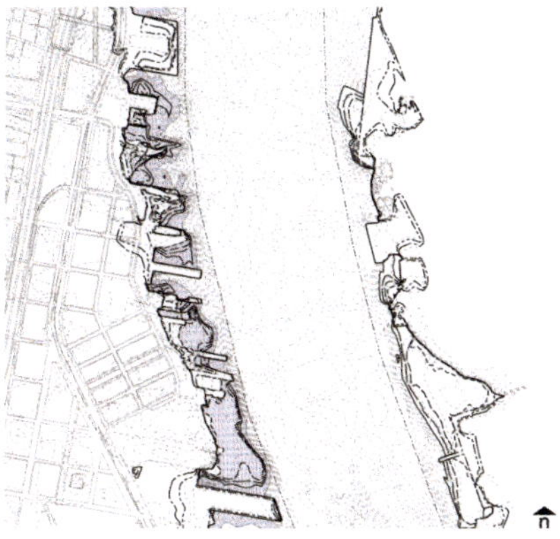

Intertidal Zones

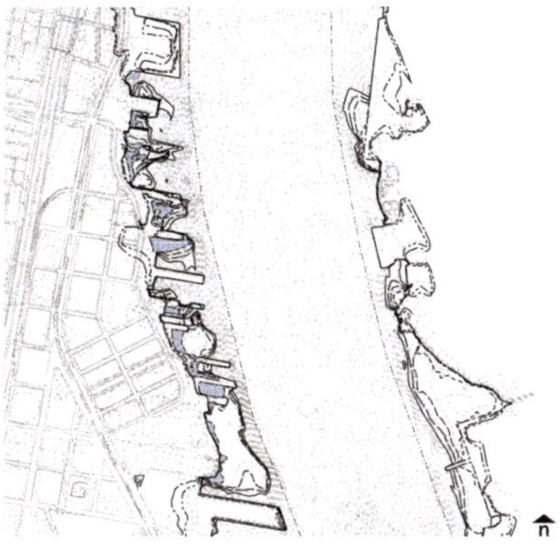

Transgression Zones

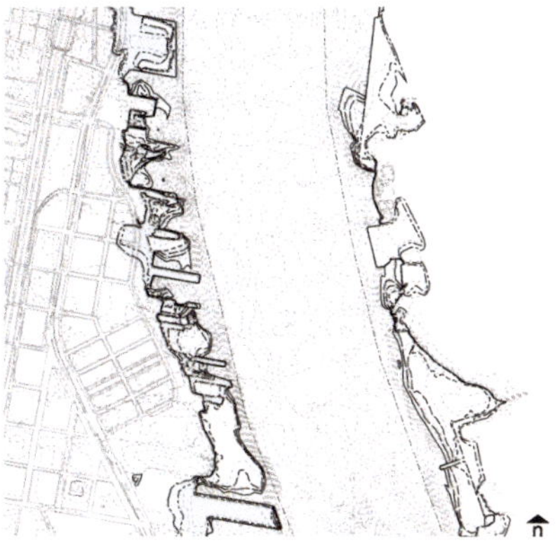

Figure 3.
GPS and depth finder on a remote control bait boat

parameters, collected and modelled through the computational capacities of geospatial analysis (GIS), computational flow dynamics and parametric software. There are two primary challenges when integrating hydrodynamic simulation into design methods: reliable data and platform interoperability.

Firstly, much of the data available for waterways are too coarse, outdated or altogether absent, since they are mapped primarily for navigation purposes. For example, a comparison of the geospatial data (topography and bathymetry) available shows that the shoreline information is missing. This is not unique to the Delaware River; these information gaps are characteristic of many urban rivers (Figure 2). This leaves data collection up to designers, which we achieved by attaching a GPS and depth-finder to a remote-controlled bait boat (Figure 3).

Secondly, it remains difficult to seamlessly transfer data among the various software platforms to create a hydrodynamic model. The collected data needs to be formatted and organised so it can be translated among analytic, simulation, and design environments. Custom scripts must be written in order to translate between platforms, which requires designers to be active tool 'makers' rather than just tool users. The data can then be analysed to understand the differential velocities and directions

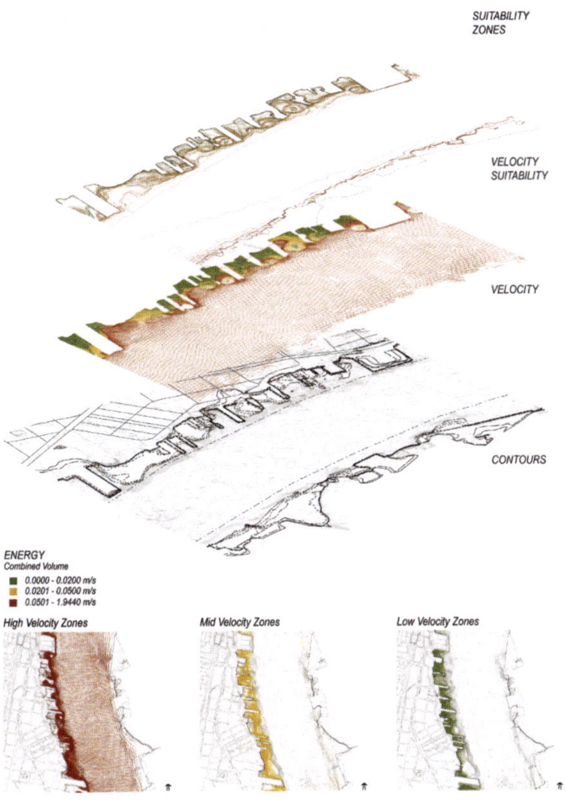

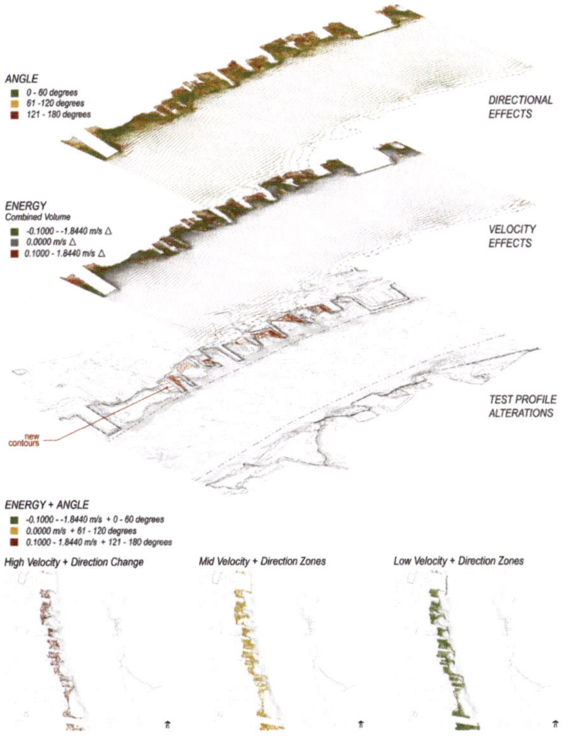

Figure 4. (Left)
Velocity, direction and elevation

Figure 5. (Right)
Profile, depth, material and alteration

along the length of the river under a variety of flow volumes and tidal heights. The velocities, directions and elevations are used to determine suitability for wetland creation (Figure 4). Any subsequent design intervention can be re-run through the simulation, under differing parameters, to see how flow responds to profile, depth and material alterations (Figure 5). While not simple, this process enables the construction of a numerically and metrically precise method that not only represents change, but also allows iterative testing of design proposals within the model.

Computer simulation offers a relational and time-dependent means for working with the dynamic material of landscape. This can enable designers to expand beyond our profession's over-reliance on illustrating change, rather than working with it. Variability and change are built into the thinking behind simulation reflecting the variability inherent to the systems they characterise. Today's design planning methods and responses should engender the same level of comfort with respect to variability and change. It is this time-dependent aspect of simulation that distinguishes it from previous modes of design. It is this aspect that makes it relevant for thinking about how we 'design with nature'[1] today.

Experiencing information

Ann Marie Schneider

INFORMATION AESTHETICS AND LANDSCAPE EXPERIENCE

From satellite images to highly sophisticated data sets, the burgeoning volumes and availability of information are shaping the aesthetics of our age. Information visualisation provides powerful analytical, creative and narrative tools that are revealing new ways of comprehending, navigating, designing and experiencing our world. These new methods hold great potential to enrich place-making, particularly for the complex, time-challenged scale of landscape.

Information aesthetics refers to the graphic representation of data, fuelled by the desire for beauty, utility and insight. Lev Manovich introduced the term "info-aesthetics" to the creative dialogue in his 2005 article The Shape of Information, making the associations between an information-driven society, the need to communicate complexity and the impact of this on form. Manovich notes that where formal qualities were "solid, stable, finite, discrete and limited in space and time, the new forms are often variable, emergent, distributed and not directly observable[1]." These same qualities are inherent to landscape as a medium: its changeability, complexity, ephemera and often non-human scales of size and time are what makes it equally fascinating and challenging.

Founded on visual communication and translation, information aesthetics has evolved rapidly over the last century. In examining the relationship of information aesthetics to the practice of landscape design, it's helpful to parse and mine the differences, similarities and interconnectedness between various types of information visualisation, particularly mapping, information graphics, data visualisation and diagrams.

Mapping is a relational operation that requires the establishment of a datum, or fixed starting point, that provides a means of measure and a visual reference. The use of maps in land planning, urban design and landscape architecture is a foundation of the practice. Geographic maps of our physical world are in daily use and allow us to contribute, as well as view, real-time data such as traffic updates, posted imagery and the latest news. However, maps can take on many forms, showing information such as the trajectories of eclipses from the fourth to the fifth century BC or the locations of cognitive functions in the human brain.

Like all aspects of information visualisation, mapping may be representational but may also be abstract, with varying degrees of agency based on the method and intent of its creator. James Corner writes that mappings are "extremely opaque, imaginative, operational instruments. Although drawn from measured observations in the world, mappings are neither depictions nor representations but mental constructs, ideas that enable and effect change[2]."

Born out of map making, information graphics are more broadly intended to convey complex information, data or knowledge through graphic means. In 1967, Jacques Bertin, a French cartographer and theorist, laid the theoretical foundation for the advancement of information visualisation in his seminal text, Semiologie Graphique (Semiology of Graphics: Diagrams, Networks, Maps). Through the logic of standard rules applied to writing and topography, Bertin methodically studied, organised and charted how we visually perceive graphic information. The result is a manual for how the graphic aspects of colour, line, form, scale, shape, texture, orientation, etc. may be most effectively utilised to communicate information.

Subsequently, the establishment of a set of rules for graphic communication meant that software could be developed, and this became the basis for Esri's GIS, founded in 1969 and now the most ubiquitous application for modelling and processing geographic and spatial data. Semiologie Graphique also provided

Newly constructed segment of the Elliott Bay Seawall, June 2015.

a foundation for the work of Edward R. Tufte, the author of several seminal books on the topic of the graphic representation of information, including Envisioning Information, Beautiful Evidence, Visual Explanations: Images and Quantities and more. Thus, Bertin's principles founded both mapping and information graphics and are used extensively to visually convey ideas.

Rooted in the mapping process, and similarly subject to graphic tenets, data visualisation involves the act of mapping data and processes to reveal patterns, structures or connections. Manuel Lima describes data visualisation as a shift away from the "19th century scientific [ ] paradigm of reduction (breaking nature into the simplest possible elements and defining rules for how these elements interact)," and a move towards "understanding the phenomena of complexity (think chaos theory, emergence, complexity theory)[3]". Theoretically and analytically, this shift is ideal for addressing landscape complexity; however, the effect of embracing complexity in landscape architectural practice and built work, where the prevailing paradigm is still that of reduction and is driven by constructability and economies of scale, remains to be seen.

Data visualisation is often perceived as more analytical and less subjective than information graphics; however, narrative plays an equal, if not a magnified role in every aspect of production. First, data input: how the data is obtained and what is gathered and from whom. Second, data processing: the criterion for data inclusion, how the data is filtered, parsed, organised, 'scrubbed' (a vernacular term used to represent the process of eliminating corrupt or inaccurate data), and any algorithms used to increase legibility. Finally, the output: the form or style of the graphic, the graphic treatments (colour, orientation, font, etc.) and even the context in which it will be presented or displayed.

Critical to generating and conveying ideas, a diagram is essentially a simplified drawing that shows arrangements and relations with the intent to explain rather than represent. In this sense, maps, information graphics and data visualisations all have the potential to serve as diagrams when they are curated to show or imply possibilities. According to architect Stan Allen:

"Although diagrams can serve an explanatory function, clarifying form, structure or program to the designer and to others, and notations map program in time and space, the primary utility of the diagram is as an abstract means of thinking about organisation. [ ] A diagram is therefore not a thing in itself, but a description of potential relationships among elements; not only an abstract model of the way things behave in the world, but a map of possible worlds[4]".

The formidable challenge of navigating and designing for the complexity of landscape, with the drive to create meaningful spaces, makes it perfectly suited for the powers of the data age and information aesthetics. Landscape's interwoven natural and anthropogenic systems, its extremes of physical scale, its vast time cycles and historical trajectories embody the new formal qualities of "variable, emergent, distributed and not directly observable[5]." Furthermore, bringing complex concepts and challenges into the realm of human understanding and experience is arguably the definition of what it means to be a landscape architect and is well-aligned with the "data visualisation artists aim [to] map [such] phenomena into a representation whose scale is comparable to the scales of human perception and cognition[6]".

Information aesthetics is most evidently used in the phases of the design process that lead up to, and inform, installation. Research, analysis, organisation and vision these landscape projects are data-driven. While most landscape architecture projects are technically data-driven from the common use of maps, GIS and diagrams, the practice is advancing into the incorporation of data visualisations. One such example is a student project on which I collaborated with teammate Meghan Storm. After obtaining an ethnobotanic data set from the University of Michigan, I created a data visualisation of plant uses by Keres-speaking Puebloans to find patterns and relationships of local plants to local culture. The visualisation provided the concept and organising principles that we used to design a housing-integrated agricultural development plan for a reservation in need of a new housing paradigm.

The role of information aesthetics in the latter phases of design are less obvious but the potential impacts on landscape spaces is an important question. How can we experience and comprehend information in the landscape, particularly in ways that don't involve an LED display or an electronic device? Datum-visualisation and data-reciprocity are two other possibilities that warrant discourse and exploration.

Datum-visualisation is the establishment and marking of references in physical space that have the capacity to impart information and assist visitors in gauging and experiencing changes to their environment. The effect is essentially to turn user experience into a real-time relational operation. Projects can range from the obvious and educational to the subtle and poetic. They may include a spatial reference, an historical trace or remnants of a process that are otherwise not visible. Notably, these interventions are also often given to artists who work alongside landscape architects in this interstitial milieu between disciplines.

One datum-visualisation example is the 'Contour Lines by the Dead Sea' project by Schlomo Aronson Architects, completed in 1996 for the Israel Ministry of Tourism. Two access highways each descend to the Dead Sea, which sits at 400 metres below sea level, the lowest point on earth. Periodically, along each road, contour lines are marked into the sides of hills by long level walls of local stone. Each wall contains a horizontal strip of blue ceramic tiles and large aluminium numbers that bear simply

1. Manovich, Lev, 'The Shape of Information', manovich.net (2005) p. 2

2. Corner, James,'The Agency of Mapping: Speculation, Critique and Invention', in Denis Cosgrove [ed.], Mappings (Reaktion Books London, c. 1999, p. 231-252) p.250.

3. Manovich, Lev, 'Forward', in Manuel Lima [ed.] Visual Complexity, Mapping Patterns of Information (Princeton Architectural Press, c. 2011, p.11-13) p.12.

4. Allen, Stan, 'Diagrams Matter', in Any 23: Diagram Work (New York, 1998).

5. Manovich, Lev, 'The Shape of Information' (2005) p. 2

6. Manovich, Lev, 'The anti-sublime Ideal in Data Art', manovich.net (2002) p.11. Note: See also response by Warren Sack, Aesthetics of Information visualisation, ucsc.edu, (c. 2007) p.2.

7. The process and video can be viewed in a series of blog posts at www.schneiderwerks.com

the contour elevation value. The visible contours enhance the dramatic descent by giving visitors a gauge by which to measure their experience and the means to view otherwise invisible information.

A more recent example is the face of the new Elliott Bay Seawall along Seattle's waterfront. A textured facade, with habitat shelves and bright yellow markings indicating high, median and low tides, is visible in the new sidewalk and wall design by James Corner Field Operations. At this time of concern for global change and sea level rise, commuters and tourists now have the ability to see finer gradations of tidal fluctuations and can relate the hourly changes in their environment to visible datums and thresholds.

Data-reciprocity refers to a landscape designed to both capture and reveal data, whether analog or digital and most of the examples of this to date are in the industrial or infrastructural, rather than the public, realm. Places such as the agricultural fields of Yuma, Arizona, are criss-crossed with complicated water infrastructure for the United States Bureau of Reclamation (USBR). A complex system of wells that monitor and record surface and groundwater conditions provide continuous data on the fluctuating water table conditions and water quality. The data is used by the USBR to operate extraction wells, diversions and irrigation channels, and water treatment facilities that support agricultural production and the water requirements with Mexico.

With the explosion of social media, data-reciprocity will find new ways of entering the landscape space. Current examples are reliant on electronic devices and applications such as PhillyTreeMap (www.opentreemap.org) where users can inventory trees in their community, log them in an open-source app and then view and search the results.

More rare, however, is the existence of data-reciprocity in the absence of immediate digital tools. Are there ways we can infuse information into our landscape without the need for an electronic device or intermediary? With this idea of analog data-reciprocity in mind, we conducted such an experiment for Park(ing) Day 2014 Seattle (an international event that allows you to co-opt a parking space for one day and turn it into a parklet). In a collaboration between Mithun and SocialScale Media, we started by gathering baseline Twitter data about Seattle's changing waterfront and its relationship to Alaskan Way (the road that divides the recreational waterfront from the historic business district). We created data visualisations of our findings, looking for clues and sentiments from which to generate ideas. Markings became traces of process - our analog data visualisation - left behind for interpretation once the site became a parking space once again. We recorded a time lapse video of these and entered the graffiti into final infographics after the event, all of which was publicly posted[7].

Whether through data-driven, datum-visualisation or data-reciprocity means, the impact of information aesthetics on landscape architecture will be of rapidly increasing significance. As translators of complex information and creators of experience, landscape architects will continue to have an expanding role in how we understand and perceive change in the world around us. The way forward lies in the undefined zones between disciplines and requires meaningful, thoughtful and direct engagement with technology, art and design to explore new landscape possibilities that can inform how we experience change.

Creative 3d mapping for design and visual representation of the landscape

Nadia Amoroso
Nadia D'agnone

"As a creative practice, mapping precipitates its most productive effects through a finding that is also a founding; its agency lies in neither reproduction nor imposition but rather in uncovering realities previously unseen or unimagined, even across seemingly exhausted grounds. Thus, mapping unfolds potential; it re-makes territory over and over again, each time with new and diverse consequences."[1]

The process of mapping has always allowed the designer to uncover visible and invisible layers of the landscape. Now, with the addition of various mapping and geo-data technologies, the power of 3D mapping has enabled designers not only to creatively display geo-information, but also to utilise the data as an instrument to design smarter landscapes and cities. These designs are backed by solid information.

GeoDesign is the term given to this new form of mapping; it is an innovative way of designing the built environment, fusing both nature and geography with design. Part of a framework that utilises GIS technology and data from the landscape, GeoDesign meshes design with value-based information to help designers, planners and stakeholders make better-informed decisions. The technology offers a set of robust tools that supports rapid evaluation of design alternatives against the impacts of those designs.

Examples of the GeoDesign approach and its technology can be seen in many of the projects of Canadian-based landscape architecture firm, O2 Planning + Design. It applied a GeoDesign approach to undertake digital terrain modelling and conceptual design in support of master planning for the Bearspaw site, a potential residential development located outside Calgary, in Rocky View County. The site itself presented many challenges, its situation being an existing quarry on a bluff east of Bearspaw Reservoir. The site required remediation of the existing quarry with new design of the landscape, possibly entailing significant earthworks. However, the site also offered many opportunities, among them a unique topography and a setting in a location with significant natural beauty. The design goal was to explore creative options to utilise the topography and overcome the challenges of redesigning the existing working landscape into a cost-effective, flexible solution that supported urban development. To meet the project requirements, O2 applied a GeoDesign approach, leveraging

Top:
Design Bearspaw, near Calgary Canada – View of South-East

Bottom:
Design Bearspaw, near Calgary Canada – View of West

Historical Iconography Image Study with Digital model superimposed on top of Iconographic View, "Catania and Etna from South-East, Anonymous, 1600-1700."

GIS as the main software and platform for analysing designs, and producing visualisations as the team explored site configuration and grading options across increasing levels of detail. This included testing various scenarios for flexible future development while testing the optimal earthwork and grading possibilities that would work with the landscape. The GeoDesign approach and technology has improved the communication of these plans to the public, offering evidence-based solutions, and the designers were able to track the project performance while better understanding the outcome of the final design.

The Anamorphic View

The principles of landscape ecology explain to us that the spatial forms, patterns and arrangements found on a site in the present are a direct result of processes of the past. As explained by D'Arcy Wentworth Thompson in On Growth and Form (1917), "... form is the diagram of force."[2] The formal composition of elements found on a site can tell us about the forces and conditions that have shaped them. This is important because it can help us gain a better understanding of the natural environmental conditions of a site prior to intervention, even those conditions hidden deep within geological time. From this perspective, the ground can therefore be understood as an autonomous, heterogeneous and formative material process, consisting of overlapped intertwined and interacting layers functioning together on various scales of time and space. The ground itself possesses an implicit structural logic that can be visually read through form.

Since the invention of the aerial view, a modern airborne subjectivity[3] has emerged in design and planning that has produced a new way of seeing from above, which has fundamentally transformed how we think, interpret, and subsequently act on the ground. The aerial view, and later the overlay method (so omnipresent and ubiquitous in design and planning today), disembody us from the ground, radically flattening its spatial, formal and temporal complexity. While the diagrams, maps and images produced by this tool reveal and visualise important regional, territorial, and environmental processes normally hidden at ground level, they do so in an incorporeal and abstract way.

The role of the ground-level view is explored in obtaining knowledge and information of the material processes that have formed, and continue to shape, contemporary urban ground through creative 3D mapping. Can the forms, patterns and processes of the ground be interpreted and studied from the ground-level view? What can be seen and how can this help us in the contemporary practice of landscape architecture? Can new ways of 3D mapping help uncover these underlying processes?

Raising questions between appearance and reality, imagination and knowledge, the notion is that the forms, patterns and processes of the geologic ground have a visual presence within the contemporary city but that they are anamorphic. The strata on the surface are incomplete, fragmented, overlapped and intertwined with one another and can therefore only be seen if looked at in the right way; through space, time, and the intertwined connections between. Through the aid of the creative cartographic techniques of mapping and diagramming, with a specific focus on 3D modelling and rendering, a methodological tool for site analysis and design is presented, exploring how we can discover more about imbricated landform processes simply by analysing form.

The methodological tool is that of an anamorphic view that traces over the otherwise unseen, invisible or unperceivable formal visual elements of the ground's forms, patterns and processes. With the cartographic tools of creative mapping, diagramming and modelling, the visual elements of form, position, scale, composition, value, colour, texture, depth, change, pattern and movement are marked out in the aerial view. These are then projected on top of a digital topographic model, and presented in perspective as seen from the ground-level view. These projections are then confronted in perspective with a series of panoramic views taken of strategically chosen existing sites to determine which, if any, of the elements are actually directly visible in the contemporary urban ground from the perspective of actual space. These operations are enabled by visualisation techniques that rely on various contemporary digital mapping and modelling technologies.

Catania Case Study

Catania, the capital city of the Province of Catania, is located on the east coast of the Mediterranean island region of Sicily, Italy. The largest community in the region, Catania is situated between the foot of Mount Etna, in the Plain of Catania facing the Gulf of Catania, and the Ionian Sea. The city is located near the boundary of the Eurasian and African tectonic plates, a zone of subduction close to the largest active volcano in Europe. The Etnean region in which Catania lies is one of the most seismic areas in all of Italy, changing both rapidly and slowly.

On a regional level, the Plain of Catania has had an important geological history and relationship to the terrestrial ground, being subject to both the alluvial deposits of the Dittaino, Gornalunga and Simeto rivers and their tributaries as well as the volcanic eruptions of Mount Etna. Mount Etna is a stratovolcano, being composed of various composite layers of its own hardened lava. These same composite layers form the contemporary urban ground of Catania. This contemporary constructed ground is a palimpsest of pre-historical, historical and contemporary archaeologies, with many strata hidden within the sedimentation and residual traces of the ground. What is visible today is but

fig.1. Base.

fig.2. Colour. Blue.

fig.3. Colour. Brown.

fig.4. Colour. Green.

fig.5. Form. Surface.

fig.6. Form. Line.

fig.7. Form. Composition.

fig.8. Texture. Pattern.

Opposite:
Valle di Bove,
Anomorphic view

one layer of a much larger succession of strata, superimposed on top of one another from various periods of time.

Testing begins with the practical task of modelling out the existing topographic relief of the entire region of the Province of Catania. Modelling here refers to both physical and digital 3D modelling of the natural landforms and topographic relief of the province of the case study region, using the Digital Elevation Model (DEM) provided by the Istituto Nazionale di Geofisica e Vulcanologia (INGV)[4]. The digital elevation model data is processed with GIS software in ArcGIS and then converted into a series of points on a Cartesian grid in the x, y and z axes, also known as a point cloud. The point cloud model is then translated into a triangulated surface mesh for further modelling and rendering purposes. This step is fundamental to the study of the ground in both urban and rural areas and is the primary tool for studying its geology, geomorphology and urbanisation patterns. Like a territorial skin or membrane, the surface produced by a terrain model gives primary information data linking regions and territories into a measurable, observational and morphological datum for further study.

The otherwise unseen visual elements of landform processes include form, position, scale, composition, value, colour, texture, depth, change, pattern and movement. These are marked out on each site from the aerial orthographic view and organised into a hierarchical taxonomy using a series of interpretive images, models and exploratory drawings. These images illustrate the visual presence of the spatial forms, patterns and arrangements that are actually visible from the ground-level view. Some elements are more obvious than others. The formal elements that are most evidently visible and telling about landform processes are those associated with the greatest topographic variation, including both changes in elevation and slope gradient. Movement is also one of the elements visibly evident but occurring less frequently. Other less conspicuous elements include surface texture and patterns, elements that read at a much smaller scale from the ground-level view.

Conclusion

The way we see and perceive the world radically changes the way we understand it and how we then act upon the ground. Through the link of the anamorphic ground-level view, the intent is to physically engage human processes within the non-human processes of the physical, biological and geological environments they inhabit.

With a clearer understanding of the importance and relevance of the physical world comes the ability to integrate sociological, political, economic and cultural elements in an intelligent way that will build lasting communities.

1. Corner, James. "The Agency of Mapping: Speculation, Critique and Invention." in Cosgrove, Denis, Mappings, Reaktion Books, 1999: p. 213.

2. Forman, Richard, referencing D'Arcy Wentworth Thompson's On Growth and Form. Found in Forman, Richard T.T., Land Mosaics: The Ecology of Regions. Cambridge: Cambridge University Press, 1995: p. 5.

3. Waldheim, Charles. "Aerial Representation and the Recovery of Landscape." in Corner, James. Recovering Landscape. New York: Princeton Architectural Press, 1999: p. 124.

4. Tarquini S., Isola I., Favalli M., Mazzarini F., Bisson M., Pareschi M. T., Boschi E. (2007). TINITALY/01: a new Triangular Irregular Network of Italy, Annals of Geophysics 50: p. 407 - 425.

Project

SENSE AND SENSIBILITIES

David Mah

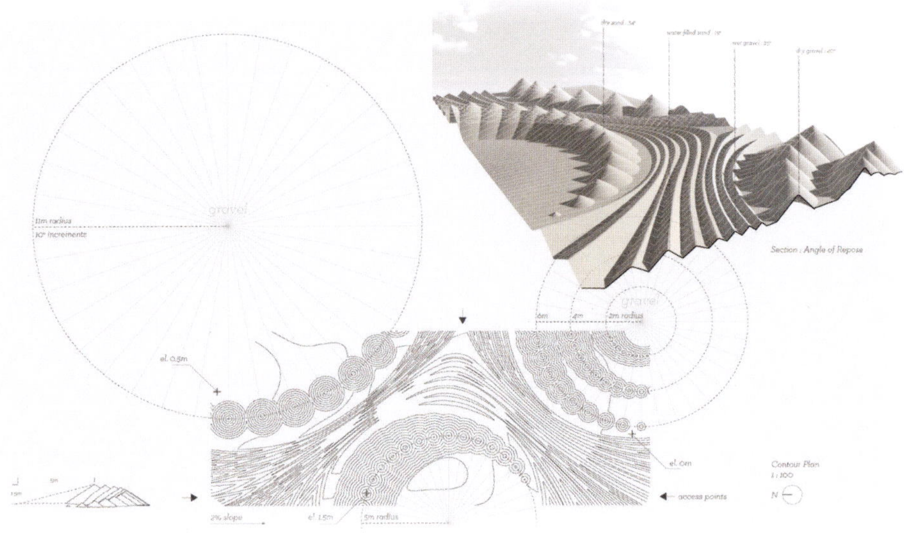

A DIGITAL SENSIBILITY OF LANDSCAPE

The contribution of the digital or, more specifically, computation, towards the disciplinary and professional concerns of landscape design, has a maturing legacy. This is tied particularly to the history of cartography and the various ways that the automated rapid processing of calculation and memory has been leveraged to order information about the world as it is. Without labouring on the actual narratives surrounding the emergence of digital mapping and GIS technologies, it is worth acknowledging this history and recognising landscape's exemplary role as an early adopter of digital technology to inform and extend its professional and disciplinary trajectory.

This legacy is symptomatic of an understanding of the profession and discipline as one that locates legitimacy for its actions in its ability to describe the world and nature as an 'authenticity', mapping existing patterns across a vast range of scales. It ties action at specific scales to wider prevailing ecological and environmental concerns. It offers a sensibility for 're-searching' and 're-presenting' the world, but can often contribute to a neglect of the practice and discipline of landscape as a projective design discipline.

It is clear that contemporary digital technology, as well as culture, has offered landscape architecture a panoply of novel means for situating its actions within the contemporary milieu and sensibility. Emerging practices include the renewal of the role of narrative in landscape design through an immersion in the new storylines that our contemporary digital culture offers, even spawning nonlinear forms of description that may stimulate the design imagination. In another spectrum, digital technology also enables an engagement with design as an explicitly material practice. It offers inventive means for articulating and configuring our material world into environments with qualities and sensibilities that communicate and engage.

For better or worse, design is in itself always a projective act: acting on the

Above:
Landform Installation generated with materially embedded form-finding algorithms.
Drawing by Michael Keller, Harvard GSD (Instructor – David Mah)

Opposite:
Expressive dune field communicating associations between hydrology with deposition and scour.
Landform model by Xinhui Li and Gege Wang, Harvard GSD (Instructor – David Mah)

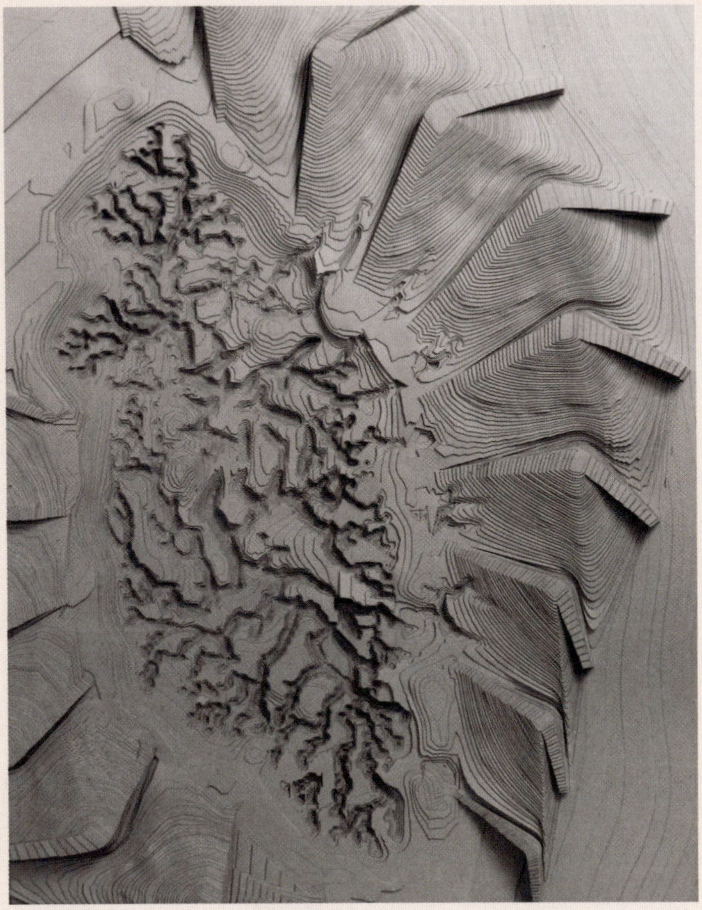

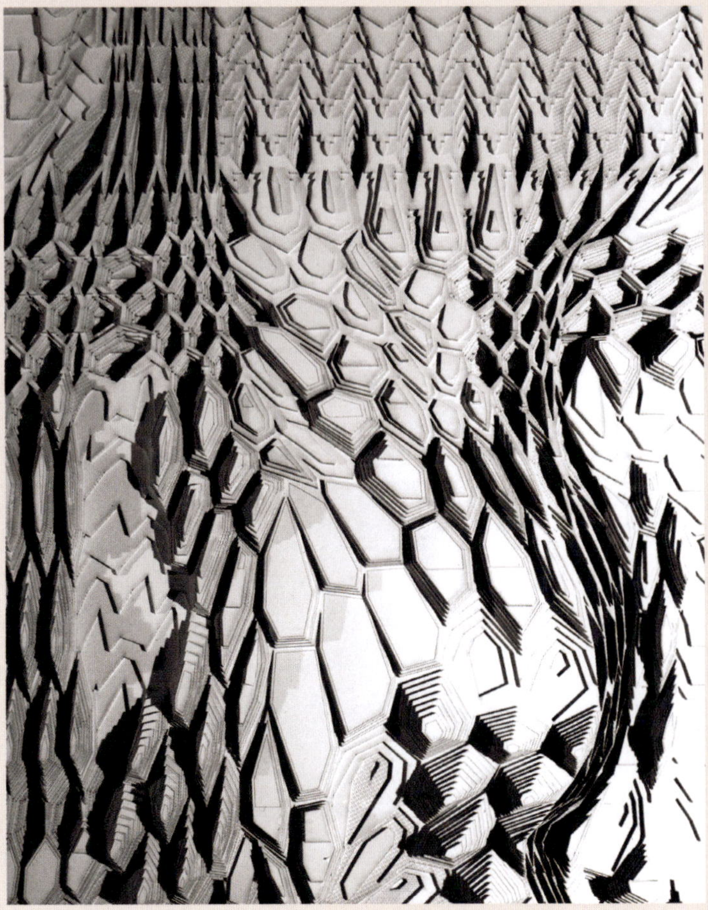

Top left:
Filtering pier array and marsh central court. Landform model by Daniel Widis and Andrew Boyd, Harvard GSD (Instructor – David Mah)

Top right:
Differentiated field of mounds and basins, a model for a novel public space type that communicates the hydrological cycle. Landform model by Elizabeth Wu and Tzy Haur Yeh, Harvard GSD (Instructor – Leire Asensio Villoria)

Bottom left:
Pier, boardwalk and dune composite landscape constructing a new public water edge. Model by Linh Pham and Jia Hu, Harvard GSD (Instructor – David Mah)

Bottom right:
Gradient deposition pattern initiated by reinforced landform field. Drawing by Zi Gu and Jisoo Kim, Harvard GSD (Instructor – David Mah).

world in anticipation of our capacity to affect, or even transform, an existing condition. Landscape is an immediately material design practice, ordering matter (both inert and biotic, and all the variations in between) into specific compositions or organisations. The disciplinary interest in leveraging landscape's temporality — its capacity for change and transformation, despite its predilection for the indeterminate and mutable — reinforces this explicitly material focus through its recent ambitions to exploit computation as a surrogate ecological clairvoyant through digital simulations. Computation, the culmination of automated calculation, memory retrieval, and capacity for both iterative and recursive operations, allows for the growing faith by the design fields in the use of digital technology to simulate and analyse material and dynamic behaviour or performance as an aid to design. Rather than generate novelty, this has reignited older design tendencies that locate the legitimacy and process of design within a form-finding process that seeks to optimise relative to a range of 'natural' dynamic or performance processes.

To extend the leverage of digital tools and culture for material practice, there is an insinuation that the design fields would do well to move beyond simply focusing on the capacity for performance and dynamic simulation associated with much of digital design's recent explorations. These approaches are, without doubt, valuable for the design process, but an over-reliance and relinquishing of design agency to these techniques betrays the same impulse for 'authenticity' embedded within a previous over-investment by the field in digital mapping. Other means of engagement with the world through material design suggests that digital technology and culture may also yield different sensibilities and other nonlinear economies of performance that could perhaps occupy a projective and propositional position for design.

In an April 2014 lecture at Harvard University's Graduate School of Design, the landscape architect James Corner articulated this corrective to the prevailing ambitions for contemporary landscape design practice. In many ways, the associated concerns of indeterminacy, flexibility and performance that have come to define the tropes of much of contemporary landscape design and discourse have, in effect, become a burdensome dogma. This is particularly true when it works to circumvent the responsibility of the landscape designer to give material shape and quality to designed environments. The blind spot of recent landscape design culture has been an engagement with the more traditional impulses of pursuing material design for its capacity to affect and invite audiences or constituents. A focus on flexibility and ecological or programmatic change has short-circuited the capacity to offer engaging spaces and environments that cultivate public interest in favour of an ever-compliant ecological and programmatic flexibility.

While benefitting from the recent research in performance and simulation through digital media, landscape design would benefit from a shift in focus towards nurturing design sensibilities and approaches. This would allow for the generation of material arrangements of aesthetic or affective value inviting public engagement. The need for a reinvestment of the material condition of our environments into spaces with public value and legibility is motivated by the growing awareness that our public and common spaces, now, more than ever, need to assume the qualities that may mobilise public engagement or articulate public concerns, rather than house a mute accommodation of flux.

Landform Modelling

A series of courses and studio projects developed at Harvard's Graduate School of Design present an approach to the definition of new public grounds that are performative yet expressive of various ecological processes. Through an engagement with associative design, aided with materially embedded digital models and various simulation

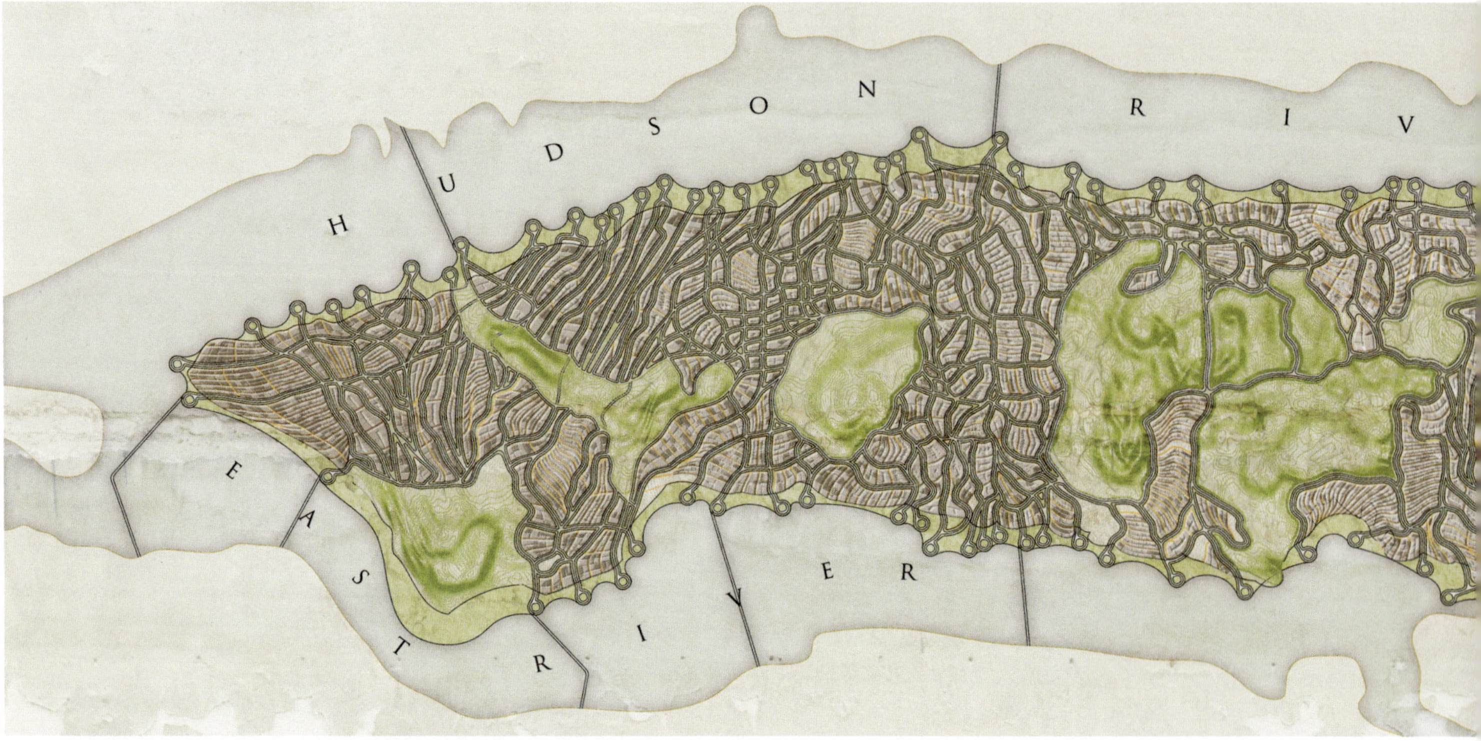

studies of ecological processes (such as hydrological and thermodynamic studies), students developed a sensibility and aesthetic for their respective projects that moved away from optimised landforms. These projects were formulated to generate material formations that make the processes of ecological flows and gradients, erosion, deposition and inundation legible and explicit. New models of public landscape invite engagement with ecological concerns that move away from the impulse to 'naturalise' that are proposed. These processes accept the opportunity to translate natural processes into deliberately communicative aesthetic sensibilities.

An Adapted Manhattan

The model of urbanisation exemplified in Manhattan's 1811 Commissioner's grid resonates with a more general categorisation of nineteenth century urban organisations that operate through a process of optimisation and regulation. Typically associated with this category of urbanisation is the synthesis of particular urban functions into replicable standards, producing a model for urbanisation that enforces an assumed formal efficiency and archetype over the particularities of a territory. The Manhattan grid also offers an exemplary capitalist model of urban flexibility, allowing for the seamless material transformation of New York through capital over time.

Manhattan's urbanisation could very well have taken a different approach, where a predecessor to the definitive 1811 plan, Mangin and Goerck's 1801 plan for Manhattan, suggests a different sensibility towards urbanisation: one which appropriates and studies existing or given conditions as the framework for its definition. Rather than an engineered exercise in optimisation based on ideal efficiencies, Manhattan's urbanisation may have evolved as a negotiation with and adaptation to the existing.

Through the analysis and reading of the site in its pre-development state, as recorded in the 1865 Viele map, the following series of speculative drawings and imagery riff off the hypothetical narrative of an alternative Manhattan

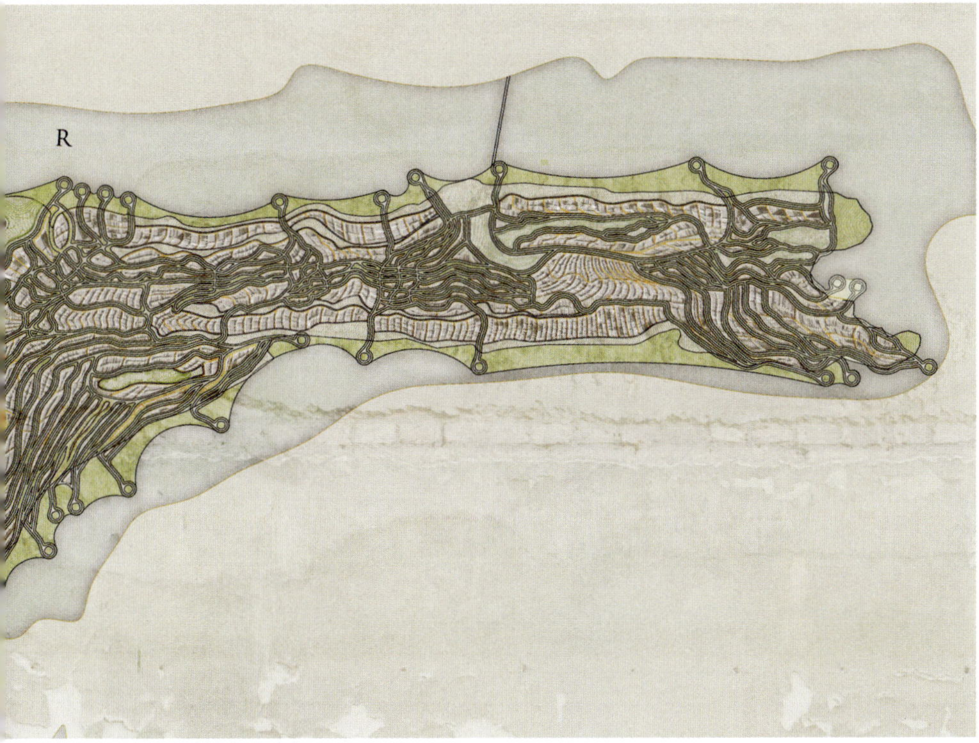

A reimagined Manhattan – reorganizing the island. Drawing by asensio_mah (David Mah and Leire Asensio Villoria) .

that emerges and evolves from both embedded and latent triggers within the site. Topography, as well as hydrological processes, offer some of the initiating patterns that reorient the simplicity of the cadastral and infrastructural grid into a highly differentiated framework for urban growth.

The relative neutrality and standardisation of the Commissioner's grid offers a model for adaptability that benefits from redundancy as well as a rudimentary formalism that supports the easy replication and repurposing of city blocks. Our speculative adapted Manhattan, on the other hand, presents an intricate ecology that invites its colonisers to identify their respective niches within its elaborate network. It visualises a tangible alternative Manhattan that communicates the impact that ecological concerns may have had on the city in place of the flexibility and seamless appropriation of the territory by the Commissioner's grid.

The formation of an infrastructural network is developed by adapting and reorienting the vectors of movement to negotiate its swelling geomorphology and to cultivate the island's surface hydrology. This reorients the development of the bundled infrastructural and cadastral grid from the actualisation of a standard idealised functionality to the possibility of an organisation that materialises from the function of adaptation. The resulting performance or functioning of this emergent organisation as a plane for colonisation no longer results from assumptions of linear relationships between form and its subsequent function, but is a by-product. It presents a conundrum in a number of parallel functional values that are often mistaken as mutually interdependent and interchangeable. The speculative re-imagination of an adapted Manhattan invites a split between these often bundled understandings of function.

FABRICATION

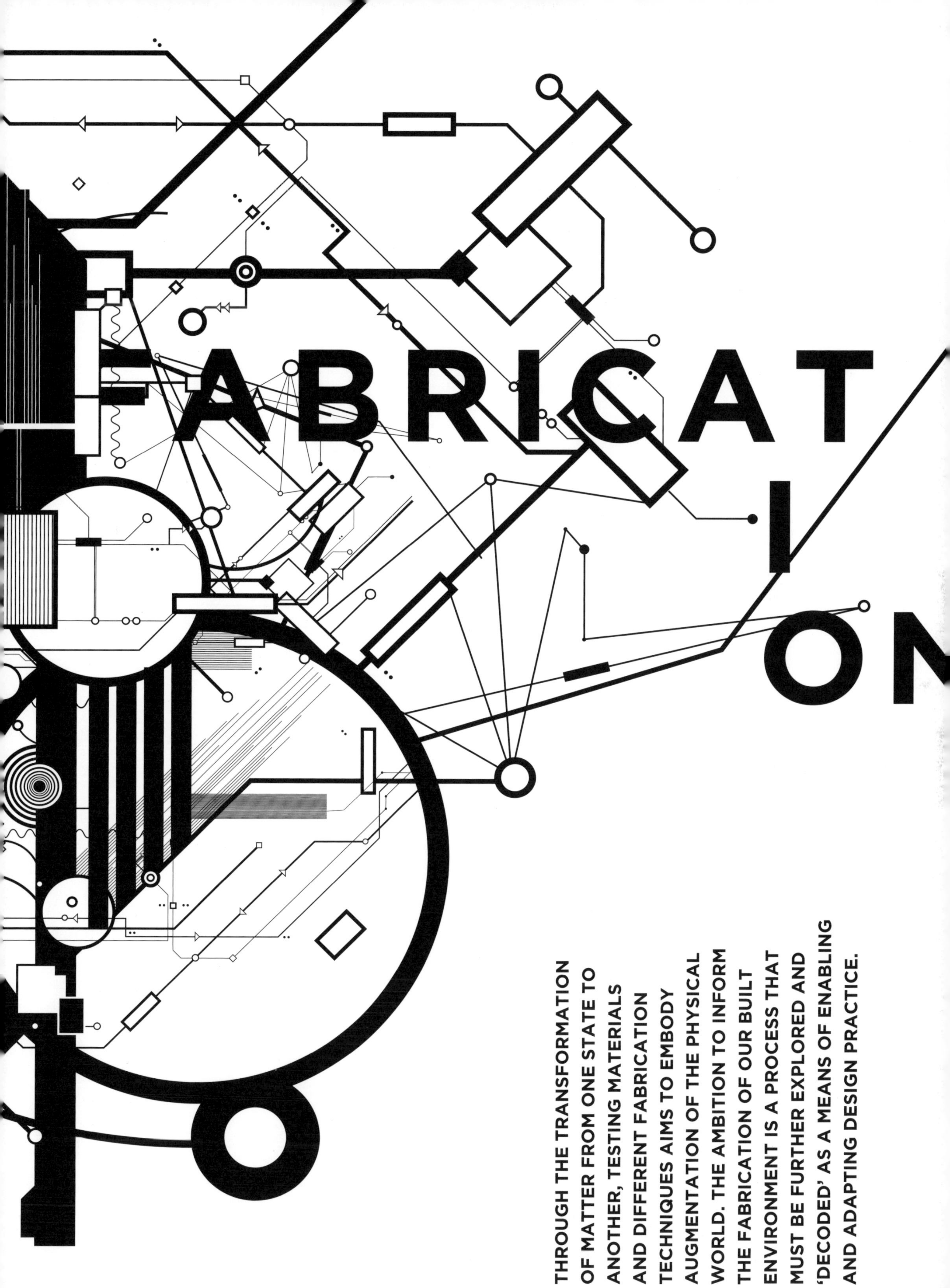

THROUGH THE TRANSFORMATION OF MATTER FROM ONE STATE TO ANOTHER, TESTING MATERIALS AND DIFFERENT FABRICATION TECHNIQUES AIMS TO EMBODY AUGMENTATION OF THE PHYSICAL WORLD. THE AMBITION TO INFORM THE FABRICATION OF OUR BUILT ENVIRONMENT IS A PROCESS THAT MUST BE FURTHER EXPLORED AND 'DECODED' AS A MEANS OF ENABLING AND ADAPTING DESIGN PRACTICE.

TOWARDS A VIRAL UNDERSTANDING OF TOOLS

SHA HWANG
GAIA SCAGNETTI

We live among digital landscapes - that much is obvious these days. The land we inhabit is digital in essence. Not only is our physical world more and more visibly shaped to host the material infrastructure that powers our digital infrastructure, but that digital infrastructure is the place where most of human action and interactions are happening.

The issue of digital landscapes in design, as a system of operations and interactions between the material and the computational, is now the default, and the condition is fascinating.

A landscape is a synthetic visualisation of the physical origin of its land modified by the human presence that inhabits it. Human cultures shape their regional landscapes, but also identify with them. Digital landscapes behave in the same way: they are shaped by the tools used to generate them and mutated by the human culture that inhabits them. Humans culturally define themselves through the digital tools they prefer to interact and design.

Taken simply, our increasing dexterity over-abstracting, modelling and simulating our environments have opened up new territories as we search for new outcomes. We cannot argue, for example, that these generative methodologies do not allow us to reach previously inaccessible (that is, inefficient) levels of complexity by hand. Nervous System, a jewellery and design studio in Boston, uses algorithmic exploration to machine complex geometries that are each unique - an artisanal outcome through algorithmic means. The recent Mcor IRIS 3D printer prints on standard sheets of paper and then glues them together, achieving the colour space of standard printing technologies in an extremely highly detailed 3D-printed form. All these are clear examples of a dimension of complexity unlocked by computational processes that generate an immense realm of new possibilities.

While most news of new tools and processes fawn over the possibilities, we find that conversation lacking. For us, it is the condition itself that should be questioned. How do these tools spread? What do we hope to gain with this increased dexterity? Are we actually augmented, or just transformed? Do all introductions of new tools create similar waves of undiscovered outcomes?

Taken further, we wish to inspect the intent of our tools themselves. If we take tools to have agency, what do our tools crave? If tools use us to enact their visions, how do our tools dream?

One way to pursue this thought is to re-discuss our assumptions on tools by imagining an alternative way to understand them. We constructed a peculiar argument: we want to depict tools as epidemic matters - tools are viruses, tools are entities that take replication as their purpose.

Viruses, of course, are organisms that infect hosts, sometimes asymptomatically, and then are spread by the carrier towards the rest of the population. Ed Rybicki, virologist and

3D-printed full colour topography by Mcor IRIS

biotechnologist, describes viruses not as lifeforms but as "organisms at the edge of life".

With this model, the manifestation of new territories and new landscapes becomes easier to understand. If tools are viruses, they are transmitted through the traces they leave in the forms we construct with them. Tools are viruses whose symptoms are form.

Though we often mock contemporary designers and architects for being too reliant on new tools, this is only natural for the infected. A viral tool has intense desires for survival, and early on they must be incredibly flamboyant in order to transmit. The double arches on display in the Great Mosque of Cordoba, the graceful bent wood of Thonet chairs or the tetrahedral truss in the various domes by Buckminster Fuller were all both formal explorations and advertisements for the tools and technologies that made them possible. Likewise, the catenary string and weight models used by Gaudi to articulate curvature and the three-point transposition tools used by Auguste Rodin's reproductive sculptor Henry Lebossé to exaggerate the dimensions of Rodin's Thinker are clear moments where the tool broadcasts its own desires through form.

Successful tools alter the DNA of entire populations through cost, materials, or even cultural attitudes around aesthetics. As tools spread, their dependence on visibility for survival lessens.

With this view, looking towards the future of tools and technologies such as computational models and simulation or 3D printing becomes not a problem of finding innovation but of finding banality - the resting state of a successful tool.

We can see this banality in the simple magic of a table by the architect Junya Ishigami. Nine meters long and almost three meters wide, the aluminum table is only 3 millimetres thick - four credit cards. Rather than a display of the infinite complexity of modelling form, or the capabilities of mass customisation, the table is a simple expression of a new banality possible with extreme precision. The angle of deflection is calculated for the aluminium sheet and is then mechanically bent in the opposite direction. This sheet, bent in much the same way as Thonet chairs, flattens when it is set down. At rest, the trace of the tools disappear. The modelling and sheet-bending tools used to produce the table become invisible to the eye but engraved in the DNA of its design.

At another scale are the 3D-printed titanium parts of the SpaceX rocket engines. Detailed, but not complex, the parts initially look as if easily made by standard CNC milling techniques. Seeing the parts as they are fabricated, however, reveals the traces of the tool. Instead of solid titanium, the interior is a dense lattice structure, making the part incredibly light. And it is in this quiet complexity that we see the true successful future of tools - creating parts that hide their lineage, taking off to spread to new worlds.

Project

PEAK EXPERIENCE

ATLAS Lab

San Francisco is defined by its hills. They give rise to, even are, its landmarks: Coit Tower, Nob Hill, the cable cars. They are the mirror image of the neighborhoods into which they divide The City. They shape the fog, guiding it away from sunny districts and into others. What better way to know San Francisco than to know its hills?[1]

Dave Schweisguth

Drawing from the nearly 53 hills that frame San Francisco's most diverse and engaging neighborhoods, 'Peak Experience'[2] reconceives the hills of San Francisco into a series of varying and undulating mounds that frame a mix of uses that promote the integration of play into traditional street models. Situated in the Financial District of Market Street, 'Peak Experience' builds upon the recreational corridor of the waterfront to establish a strong identity for Market Street. The augmentation of the flexible sidewalk zone creates an active corridor that supports interactive discovery, play and community engagement. Responding to often static streetscape elements, 'Peak Experience' proposes a soft and flexible sidewalk zone that seeks to introduce a malleable street typology that provides a platform for varying community experiences, while educating visitors about San Francisco topography.

1. Schweisguth, Dave. "How Many Hills of San Francisco?" SFGazetteer.com: Bits of San Francisco Geography.

2. The project title, 'Peak Experience' is from Tom Graham's 2004 SFGate's article that investigates and highlights the famous hills of San Francisco.

1 THE SETTING

San Francisco is the City of Hills

San Francisco's iconic and majestic terrain is comprised of 53 hills and has curated the City's most vibrant and diverse neighborhoods .

2 THE SITE

Market Street lacks views of San Francisco's iconic landscape

Situated along the "flats" of San Francisco, Market Street provides direct access to SF's diverse neighborhoods, yet lacks visibility to the hills that frame the City and does not support a vibrant platform for community engagement.

3 THE OPPORTUNITY

Topography is an agent for interactive discovery, play + engagement

The Market Street corridor has the opportunity to integrate interactive play by means of deploying San Francisco's playful topography as an agent for interactive discovery, play and engagement along Market Street's flexible sidewalk zone.

4 THE VISION

Establish a unique cultural corridor for Market Street

Establish a flexible, educational, and culturally unique recreational corridor for Market Street that provides a diverse platform for community engagement.

Below:
Prototype programming

Following pages:
Peak Experience installation images

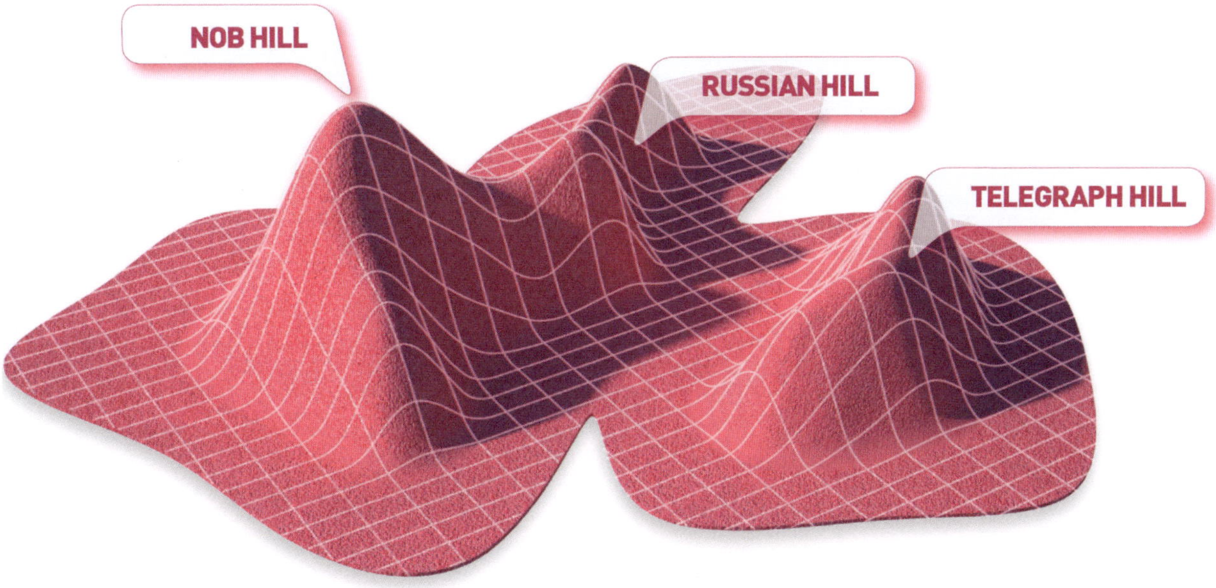

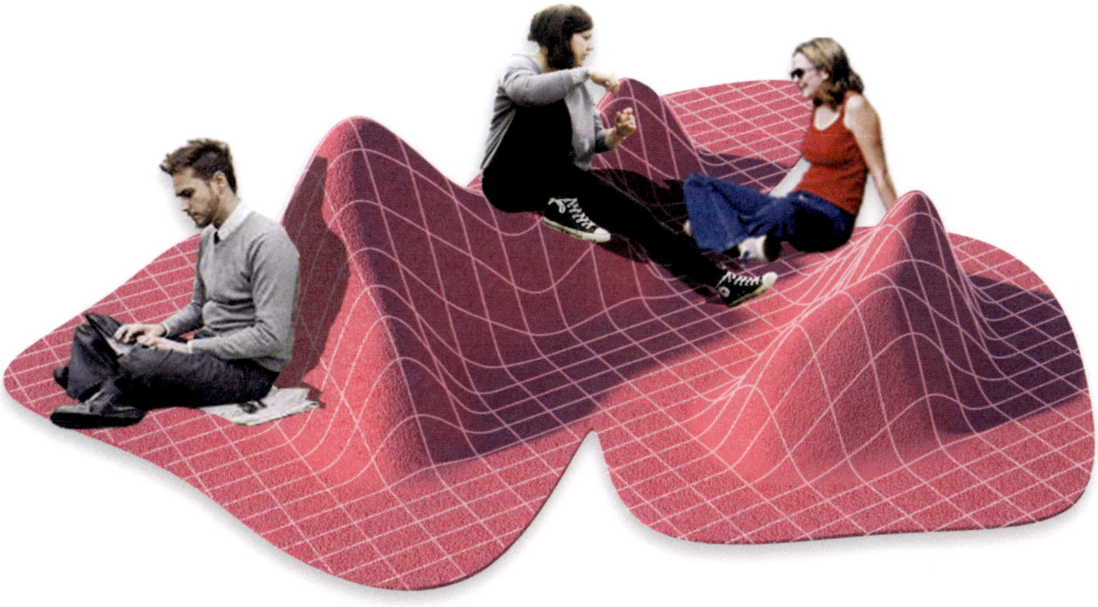

575
MARKET
+240'
NOB HILL

MARKET

555
+240'
300'

Left:
Minimaforms at
Petting Zoo

Opposite:
Vehicle

A Conversation with : MINIMAFORMS

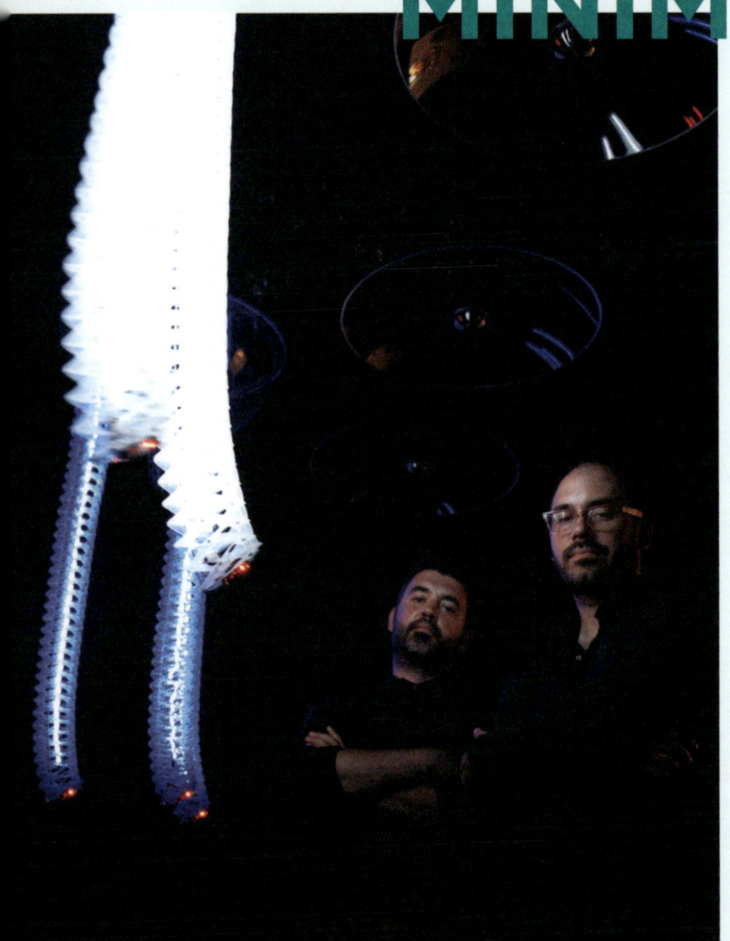

Minimaforms is focused on techniques designed to challenge the existing ideas of communication and human interaction. Through the transformation of matter from one state to another, testing materials and different fabrication techniques aims to embody augmentation of the physical world to encourage deeper connections beyond just the tactile.

Opposite top and botom:
Budapest Museum of Light

Following pages:
Soft Cast

Do you think that technology as a human pursuit has the capacity to directly influence and affect behaviour? To what extent have your projects exemplified new methods of interaction and communication?

Yes, we believe it does ... Technology for us is a very human pursuit. It is an enabling agency that necessitates an active intellectual, cultural and social enquiry. Our Petting Zoo project is not pessimistic or optimistic, it is exploring artificial intelligence and robotics and the emotive relationships that can be fostered between humans and machines within an environment. We are exploring behaviour.

When exploring methods of fabrication, what factors influence the translation and production of your designs?

This varies from project to project. We have always believed in an active engagement in design research that explores making and new methods of fabrication. Making, for us, is an active form of thinking and enables us to experiment and realise our work through prototyping everything from atmospheres and soft robotics, to rethinking the use of textiles for fabric-formed soft cast strategies. Over the last five years, in particular, we have worked in the studio on a diverse range of scales and challenges. These have included a 766-acre master plan for Athens National Park, designed by Renzo Piano, where we were commissioned to design the illumination for the park and two pier-situated thematic landmarks, to developing our emotive robotics interests in projects such as the Petting Zoo. Our approach towards production challenges – in a creative manner – complex design problems. Sometimes that is working with industries that can assist in non-standard design solutions such as shipbuilding fabricators that we are using in Athens, or inventing new techniques for deployable architectures that you can take with you as in the work we are developing in Norway. We have been developing a generative patterned textile that can deploy as a fabric in a tensile tent-like structure that, if need be, can later be solidified through casting it in concrete or with compacted earth. Research like this uses the opportunity given to us to construct a land-art intervention in Norway to prototype this research experiment full-scale.

Our research for this project is part of a larger agenda towards applications such as post-disaster scenarios and the need for us to participate in complex problems and offer alternative solutions to the challenges that are demanded. A half-scale wall section prototype was recently shown at the FRAC Centre for Art and Architecture in Orleans, France.

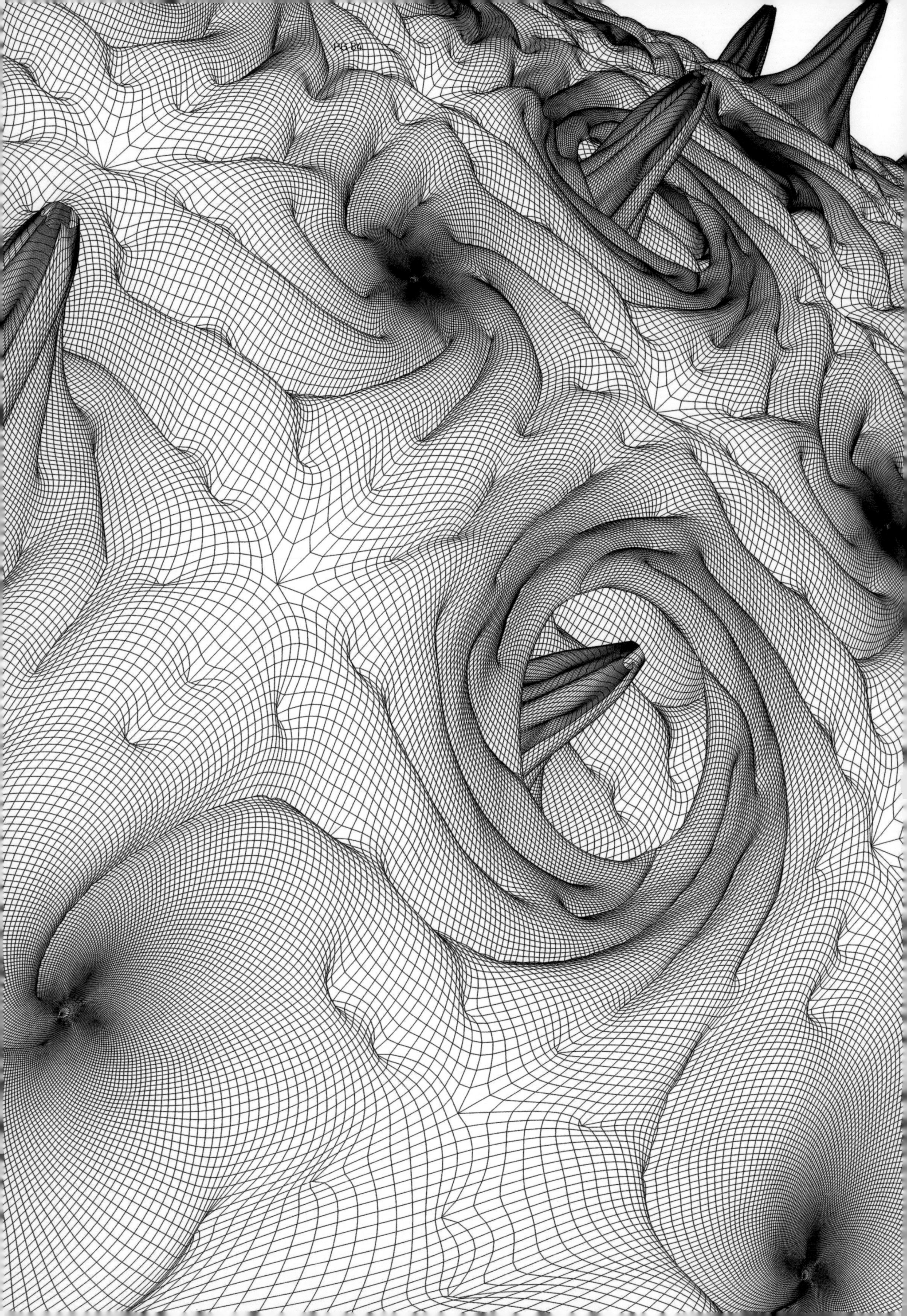

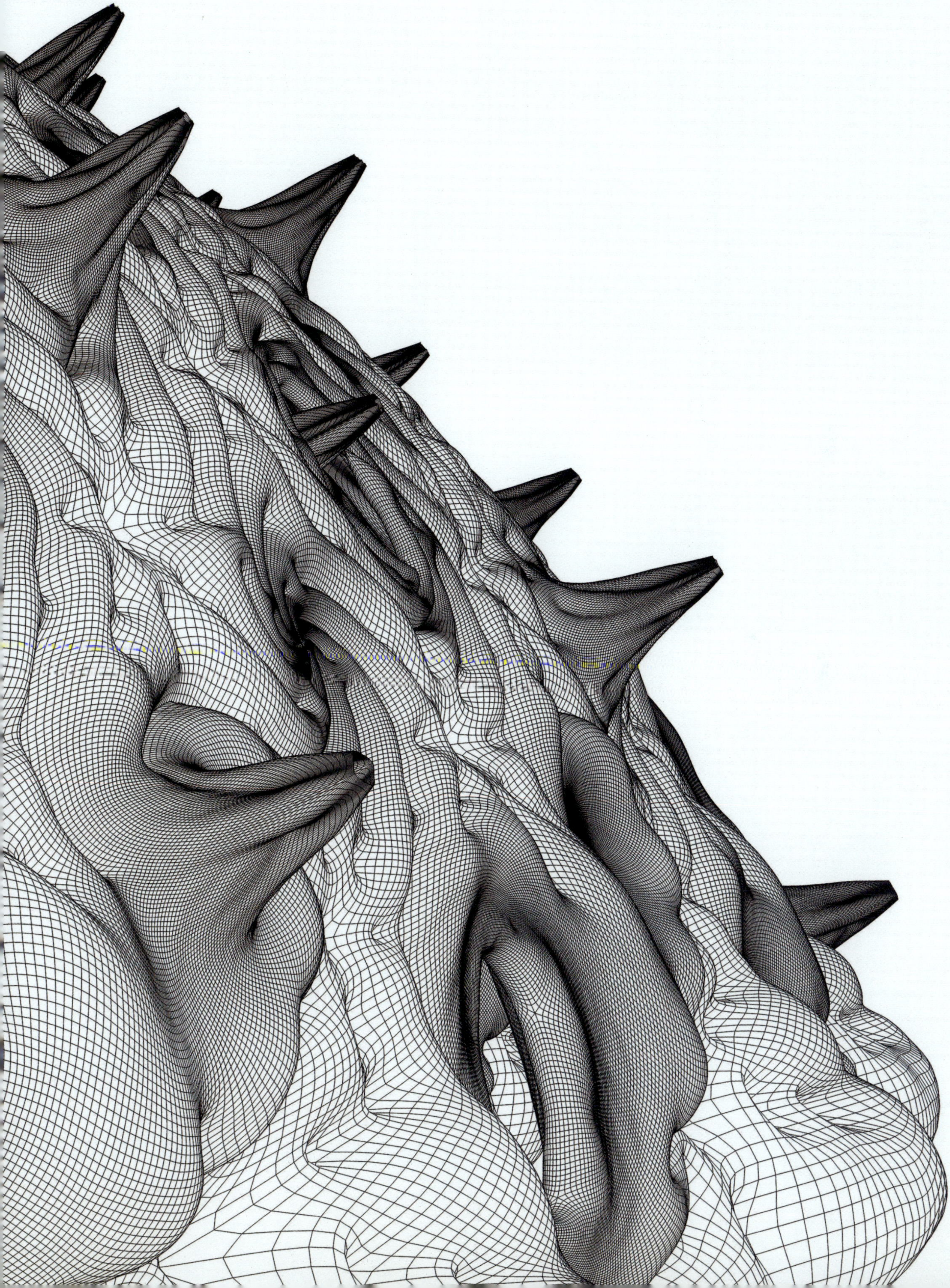

Opposite:
Emotive City

How does the process of evolution beyond form and beyond computation impact your approach to discovering new materials?

We examine an active and engaged approach towards what we have described as a behavioural model for design. Stephen and I are very much interested in the interaction of things and how this constructs an approach that redefines our relationship to matter, machines and people. Our interest was, and remains, to move beyond models and methods that reinforce the fixed and finite and embrace an approach towards design that is dynamic and evolving. We do not believe in disciplinary distinctions within design. These distinctions for us are artificial and we have pursued projects without categorisation regarding our response. This has allowed us to develop a diverse body of work over the years that has ranged from interfaces, landscapes, vehicles, atmospheres and buildings, through to master plans.

Design is our mode of enquiry to ask more informed questions of how to operate, challenge and redefine convention. Progress is about enabling, in particular, the practice of architecture and design to evolve and to actively participate in ongoing issues. Design does not have a finite definition — it is an environment for intellectual and spatial interrogation. We have to situate and contextualise our ability to define, communicate and make accessible. Design, in all forms of creative practice, has to be dynamic and evolving, to deal with ways of addressing time, latency and uncertainty.

We believe in participatory and enabling models of design that allows people the opportunity to actively influence and shape their environment. We want our environments to evolve lifelike attributes that engage the everyday and stimulate our interactions with each other. We believe that design should account for uncertainty and the unknown, to develop an approach that will allow for adaptation and evolution. Our work is time-based and scenario driven. To do this, we employ a working methodology that explores generative forms of practice within social and material agency. All is interaction.

What new approaches to the physical manifestation of material have you adopted in your experiences with fabrication processes?

There are some clear approaches that have manifested in three strands of explorations within our work. The first looks at communication as a model of interaction between things. This is present in our installation work and public interventions. Within this world our interests lie in enabling participation, making work that explores aspects of emotive design through behaviour. We examine durational approaches towards designed environments.

The second is developing methods to build performative structures that are deployable, reconfigurable and deal with complex geometries. These move beyond form towards formational strategies, which examine issues of mobility, radical reconfiguration, material life cycles and phase change. Within this research we explore materiality, programmable matter, generative design and agent based organisational strategies.

The third strand is speculative research within the world of self-aware, self-assembled and structured environments. This work looks towards reconsidering robotics and soft systems within a larger ecology of man/machine ecologies. An example of this can be seen in our Nesta commission called 'Emotive City' and the work that we develop with our students at the AADRL Spyropoulos Design Lab.

Above:
Memory Cloud Detroit

Below and opposite:
Electric Garden

To what extent have your projects exemplified new methods of interaction and communication?

Our projects examine communication as the enabling agency for all forms of interaction. The move towards making things more shared and collective also encourages people to really engage with things. That level of engagement is very important to us.

What we mean by this is most clearly demonstrated in our work 'Memory Cloud' that was performed in London's Trafalgar Square in 2008, and outside the Detroit Institute of Art in 2011. 'Memory Cloud' created a dynamic hybrid space that communicated personal statements as part of an evolving text, animating the built environment through conversation. Interaction was facilitated through mobile phones allowing for an open, personal and accessible medium for exchange. The power of this project was to examine communication and the city as a canvas for collective expression. In Detroit, a light biennale which has had two cycles, most recently in September 2014, was inspired by 'Memory Cloud' and has grown to include 30 local and international artists using the city as a medium to collectively bring the community together to see their city anew.

Other works, like Petting Zoo, are the speculative life-like robotic environment that raises questions of how future environments could actively enable new forms of communication with the everyday. Artificially intelligent creatures have been designed with the capacity to learn and explore behaviours through interaction with participants. Within this immersive installation, interaction with the pets fosters human curiosity and play, forging intimate exchanges that are emotive and evolving over time. Beyond technology the project explores new forms of enabled communication between people and their environment.

Project

IOGRAPH

Elle Stephenson

In a world of pervasive information, we are bound by signals, symbols and connections. Everything that surrounds us can be quantified, measured, analysed and permanently stored, indicating a shift in the human condition[1].

IOGRAPHICA aims to decode and translate different modes in which data can be made visible. By creating time maps of mouse activity via the application IOGraph, the work considers mapping time by creating abstract digital landscapes. The drawings illustrate themes of connectivity and dispersal. To visualise and expand movement on a small as well as large scale simultaneously I have translated the diagrams onto a wall.

The experiment is realised through pencil drawing, a material that provides a new interpretation. The objective of the expansion of the map is not only to encapsulate the polarity of scale but also to draw attention to the actual act of mapping. Creating graphic representations of information by using spatial relationships within the graphic to represent relationships between the data, irrespective of the source map, the physical process becomes a form of mapping in itself. The work aims to be a tangible representation of the physical activity of mapping virtual data and digital landscapes. The result of the work asks questions about permanence, especially because of its form. Drawing, commonly associated with the portrayal of fixed representation, draws attention to the static quality of the work. This is challenged by the interactive presence of the IOGraph program that concurrently plays alongside the material form. The program also tracks the amount of time lapsed, revealing the temporality of the work and thus creating a clash in the ratio of time - in a macro and micro sense.

Opposite:
Interactive presence of the IOGraph program that concurrently plays alongside the material form

1. The Art of Data | Aspen Ideas Blog. 2015. Available at: http://www.aspenideas.org/blog/art-data.

Creating representations of information using spatial relationships.

AUGMEN
TA

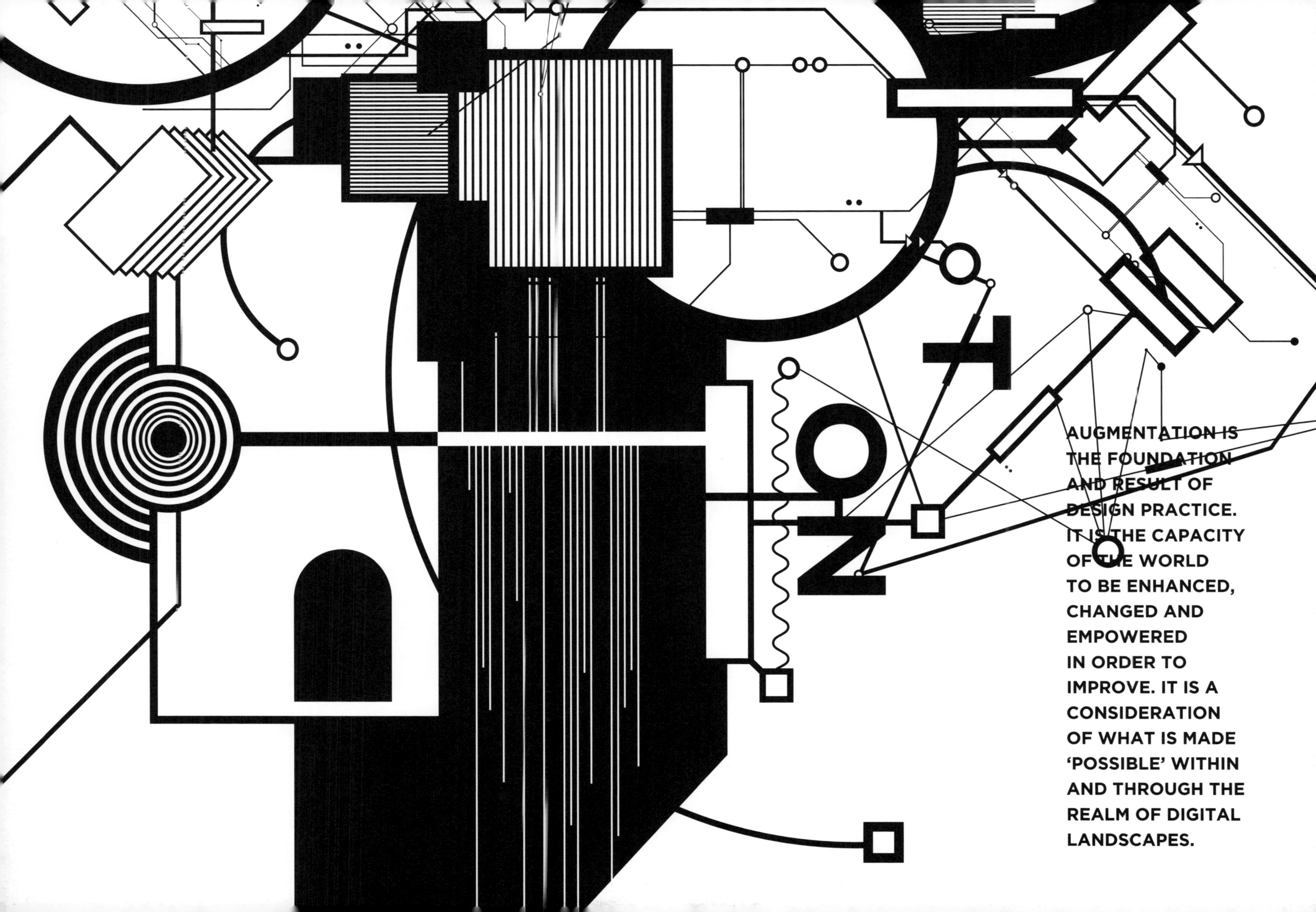

AUGMENTATION IS
THE FOUNDATION
AND RESULT OF
DESIGN PRACTICE.
IT IS THE CAPACITY
OF THE WORLD
TO BE ENHANCED,
CHANGED AND
EMPOWERED
IN ORDER TO
IMPROVE. IT IS A
CONSIDERATION
OF WHAT IS MADE
'POSSIBLE' WITHIN
AND THROUGH THE
REALM OF DIGITAL
LANDSCAPES.

Vivid Latency

Jack Isles
Dongsei Kim

DIGITAL EXPLORATIONS ACROSS THE AUSTRALIAN OUTBACK

Throughout the nineteenth century, environmental determinism shaped global attitudes towards spatial occupation. In a time in which the earth's hidden secrets were read through the undulation of its surface, spatial organisation of man was largely explored through the cartographic lexicon of geography. Towns and cities were thought to have been swept like sand into vast dunes of urbanity, resting in the cradle of a resource-abundant ecology. However, the expanding physical imprint of urbanisation saw the proliferation of economic, political and social considerations into a multifaceted definition of spatial dynamism. Yet at some point during this Vidalian reflection, the development of geography gave way to geology, and our tools of observation began to trace the unknown.

The Eye That Blinds Us

Since the conception of visual representation, architecture has been dictated by methodologies of perception. However, long before the perspectival revolution, humankind expanded its imagination through the instruments of geometry and geographies. Nevertheless, Juhani Pallasmaa writes on the shift towards the hegemony of the eye since humankind's migration from the spoken to the written mode[1]. The technologies of our time have since shaped tools of representation and thus sculpted the means through which we imagine our occupation of the lithosphere.

The perspectival revolution during the Renaissance saw a radical shift in the way architecture was imagined and represented. Christian Ganshirt describes perspective as one of the key discoveries of the modern age, formulating "... generally valid, empirically sound rules that allowed anyone applying them to depict three dimensional situations." Ganshirt further writes: "... seeing in perspective became the basis of a completely new understanding of space and landscape that shaped the art, architecture and science of subsequent centuries"[2]. The more significant aspect of this representational revolution was in that perspective was now considered to be a scientific tool, and one that can be 'objectively' deployed.

Hashim Sarkis, in his essay The World According to Architecture, defines the pedagogical effect of geography and geometries as:

"... the history of geography is strongly linked to the history of discovery and colonization. The instruments for the discovery of territory were extended into its documentation and then, in turn, into its appropriation and transformation[3]".

This expounds the fact that it has not simply been the earth's surface that determinates its occupation, but the means through which we represent and exploit it. Then what are the dominant technologies of our time that dictate the conventions of our spatial configuration?

Over the last few decades, acceleration in technological leaps in Geographic Information System (GIS) and Global Positioning System (GPS) combined

Opposite:
The eyes of the Pilbara penetrate deep beneath its ochre crust. Through mapping these trajectories we find newfound lineage between its deepest geologies and the skies above

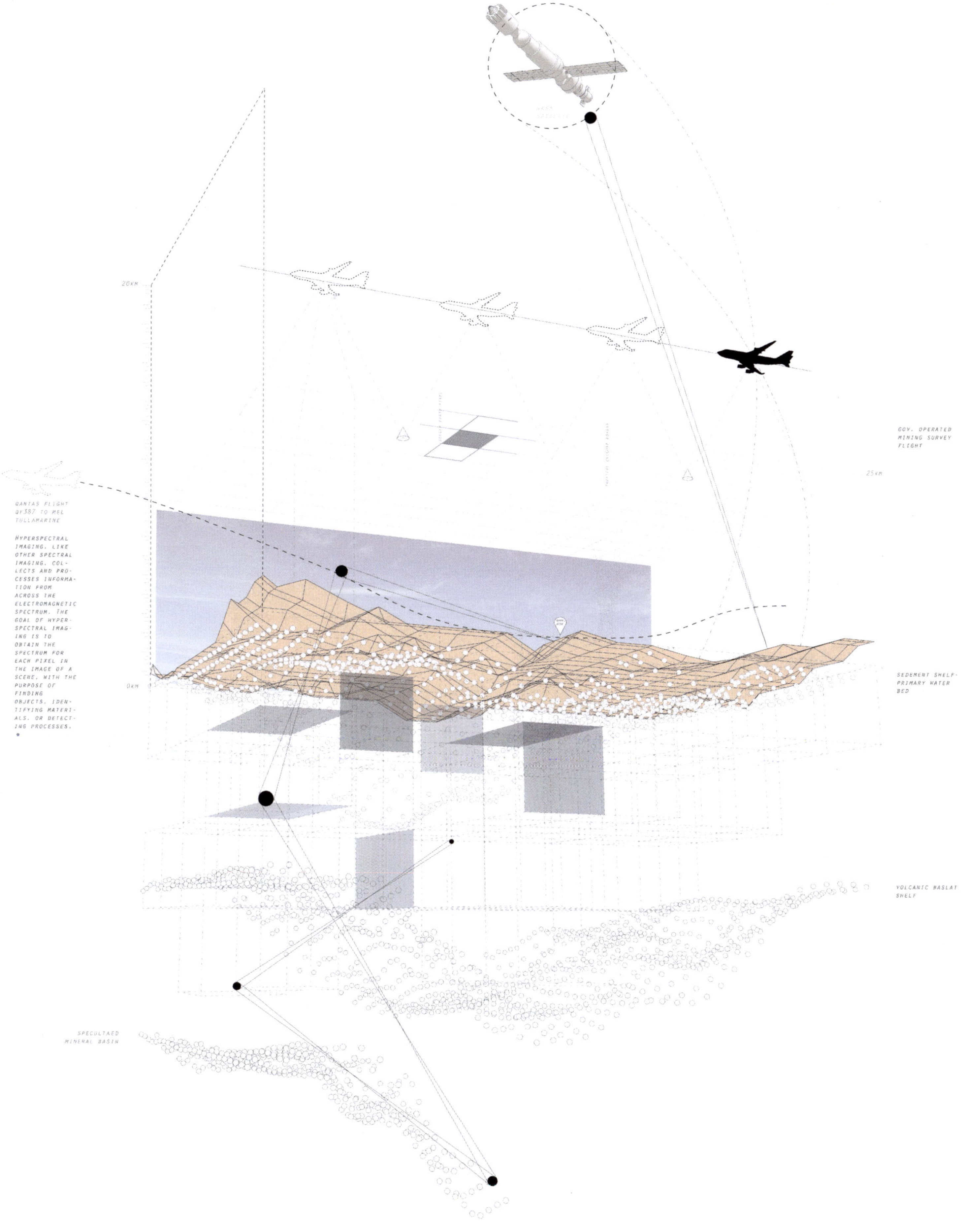
20KM
GOV. OPERATED
MINING SURVEY
FLIGHT
25KM
QANTAS FLIGHT
QF387 TO MEL
TULLAMARINE
HYPERSPECTRAL IMAGING, LIKE OTHER SPECTRAL IMAGING, COLLECTS AND PROCESSES INFORMATION FROM ACROSS THE ELECTROMAGNETIC SPECTRUM. THE GOAL OF HYPERSPECTRAL IMAGING IS TO OBTAIN THE SPECTRUM FOR EACH PIXEL IN THE IMAGE OF A SCENE, WITH THE PURPOSE OF FINDING OBJECTS, IDENTIFYING MATERIALS, OR DETECTING PROCESSES.
0KM
SEDEMENT SHELF-
PRIMARY WATER
BED
VOLCANIC BASLAT
SHELF
SPECULTAED
MINERAL BASIN

with 'big-data,' 'geodesic point-cloud techniques,' 'crowdsourcing data collection' and the rise of the internet have engendered a new world view for humanity. These new technologies combined afford humanity new ways of seeing, and thus understanding, each other and how the site is defined. A powerful example of this is extensively illustrated in Denis Cosgrove's Apollo's Eye. Cosgrove writes about a series of NASA's first photographs that captured the entirety of the earth floating in the vast universe, taken from Apollo 8 in 1968 (Earthrise) and Apollo 17 in 1972 (Blue Marble). These images contributed to a significantly "altered image of the earth", further engendering a cosmopolitan world view that was without "all those differences and nationalistic traits[4]". However, in an age driven by dependency on its own global systems of resource extraction and its consumption, it is our exploration below that has come to define much of our world today.

Perception of Depth

At its highest point Mt. Meharry (1249 metres) surveys the low-slung mining fields of Western Australia's Pilbara, an area more than 500,000 square kilometres, roughly the size of Spain. Embedded within what is thought to be the world's oldest geological member, vast mineral deposits bend and curb beneath the adjacent earth. These fertile soils rich in gold, copper, zinc and nickel have become home to a network of rails, roads and cities that in 2013 generated a twenty per cent share of the global steel market. Dotted across the land, each city and its associated parts form an intricate mechanism of logistical distribution, instrumental in its own territorial division. However, its spatial configuration is not only determined "by new industrial forms based on global supply chains[5]", but also the means through which we measure its subsurface, thus dictating the new lithospheric inscriptions.

As the global reach of planetary urbanisation extends both horizontally and vertically, transcending its own hemispheric borders, it is not only geography but deep geology that drives our spatial distribution. Now an industry standard in geological mapping, point cloud technology has universally changed the way we perceive geology.

Opposite:
Human's spatial occupation dictated by the global reach of planetary urbanisation extends both horizontally and vertically. The shipping channels of the Pilbara's Port Headland inscribe upon the waters surface the ebb and flow of its digital landscape.

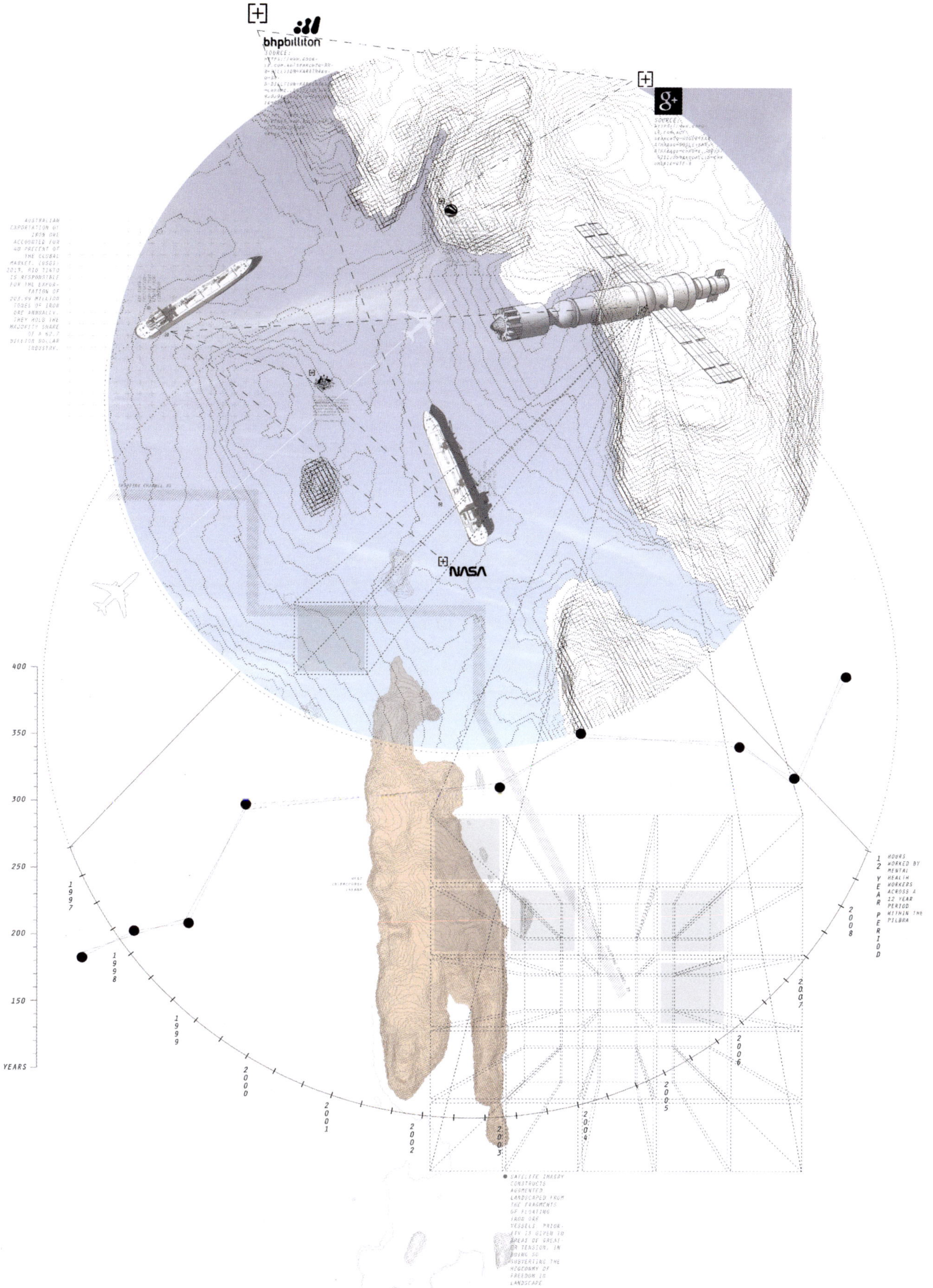
bhpbilliton
SOURCE:
AUSTRALIAN EXPORTATION OF IRON ORE ACCOUNTED FOR 40 PERCENT OF THE GLOBAL MARKET. (USGS) 2013. RIO TINTO IS RESPONSIBLE FOR THE EXPORTATION OF 203.99 MILLION TONES OF IRON ORE ANNUALLY. THEY HOLD THE MAJORITY SHARE OF A 62.7 BILLION DOLLAR INDUSTRY.
SOURCE:
NASA
400
350
300
250
200
150
YEARS
1997
1998
1999
2000
2001
2002
2003
2004
2005
2006
2007
2008
12 YEAR PERIOD
HOURS WORKED BY MENTAL HEALTH WORKERS ACROSS A 12 YEAR PERIOD WITHIN THE PILBRA
SATELLITE IMAGERY CONSTRUCTS AUGMENTED LANDSCAPED FROM THE FRAGMENTS OF FLOATING IRON ORE VESSELS. PRIORITY IS GIVEN TO AREAS OF GREATER TENSION, IN DOING SO SUBVERTING THE HEGEMONY OF FREEDOM IN LANDSCAPE

Capable of rapidly merging different scales of information, point cloud technology can "develop large-scale landscape projects while maintaining a positive feedback loop that remains true to GPS coordinates[6]". Consequently, the precision and detail of these digital technologies have made them the primary agents in geological exploration and the Pilbara's urban configuration. They are temporary outposts that define the cities' edges, swell in flux, parallel to the economy. These temporary camps, which house the miners, reflect the technological dynamism of the digital flows that define them. Shifts in market value, based on readings of the earth, thus dictate the volume of these outposts, determining the definition of the Pilbara's population. The rails, roads, ports and towns mobilise to service a new urban model, based upon its own rapid digital computation. Across the Pilbara, scarification of the earth becomes a trend-line or bar chart inscribed onto our lithosphere, narrating its own story through the eyes of technology. Nevertheless, human's spatial occupation and experience is an absent driver in these settlements.

These spatial arrangements are configured for maximum efficiency in resource extraction, often not grounded in the earth, but closer to the 'Digital Landscapes' below.

Latent, embedded within the matrix of the point cloud, lie the fabric of our cities and the coordinates of our future. Scattered throughout the skies above the Pilbara, satellites, planes and other aerial apparatus scour the surface for any geographical irregularity. These eyes of the city, lost in perpetual reflection, bring forth the information that defines its occupation. Both satellites and survey planes feed the point cloud through the collection of Hyperspectral Imagery. By capturing the earth's electromagnetic field Hyperspectral Imagery can analyse "each pixel in the image ... with the purpose of identifying materials[7]". Subsequently, each pixel holds within it both a value and location, and from this we draw the road map of our urban inhibition.

1. Pallasmaa, Juhani, The Eyes of the Skin: Architecture and the Senses. Hoboken, NJ: John Wiley & Sons. 2005, p. 11.

2. Gänshirt, Christian, Tools for Ideas: An Introduction to Architectural Design, Berlin: Birkhäuser, 2007, p. 163, p. 164.

3. Sarkis, Hashim,"The World According to Architecture: Beyond Cosmopolis", in New Geographies: Scales of the Earth, Vol. 04. (2011), p. 107.

4. Denis Cosgrove, Apollo's Eye: A Cartographic Genealogy of the Earth in the Western Imagination, Baltimore: Johns Hopkins University Press, 2001, pp. 257-8.

5. Charles Waldheim and Alan Berger, Logistical Landscapes. Landscape Journal vol. University of Wisconsin Press 2008, p. 1.

6. Christophe Girot, "Scales of Topology in Landscape Architecture", in New Geographies: Scales of the Earth, Vol. 04. (2011), p. 156

7. Wikipedia, "Hyperspectral-Imaging". http://en.wikipedia.org/wiki/Hyperspectral_Imaging. Accessed 1 May 2015.

8. Christophe Girot, "Scales of Topology in Landscape Architecture", in New Geographies: Scales of the Earth, Vol. 04. (2011), p. 161.

9. Hermann Vaske, Standing on the Shoulders of Giants, Berlin: Die Gestalten Verlag, 2001, p. 112.

Drawing the Horizon

The Pilbara presents a unique, however not unprecedented, model for a new type of spatial determinism, dependant on its own tools and technologies of representation. Christophe Girot, Chair of Landscape Architecture at Swiss institute ETH, describes the prevalence of digital technology in the fabrication of our architecture as thus:

"In a field of work where 2D layering, projection, and zoning were the rule in the twentieth century, we have now entered an age where geo-referenced 3D visualizing has become the state of art and an absolute necessity of the dynamic modelling of large-scale projects[8]".

Therefore, has our occupation of the earth become prescribed through the language of our very own 'Digital Landscape'?

We are blind without all the proliferating digital instruments in an age driven by the precision of technological observation. Ironically, these new vivid views, produced by advanced imaging technologies, are so stimulating they can be blinding, often at the expense of phenomenological factors. This creates a swathe of blind spots, harder to consciously notice. Upon historical reflection, we know that it is our ability and extent to which we can imagine that defines the architecture of our cities, and without its technology we are blind. Latent within the network of our spatial organisation lies the narrative of our past and the atlas of our future. The 'Digital Landscapes' emended within our systems of global observation have therefore begun to augment a new contemporary framework of modern urbanisation. Neil French once noted: "We are slowly becoming aware that we cannot just photograph reality with a camera, but that it can actually create reality[9]". As we examine the world through the eyes of our cities, it is the 'digital' landscapes that define those of our future.

Project

THE DATA DRIVEN DRIVE

Greg Dahlke
Abram Elbersohn

Opposite:
Figure 1.
Computer-driven equipment customizes irrigation fertilizer application rates.

Below:
Figure 2.
Herd tracking

The United States is one of the leading agricultural producers in the world, with over 330 million acres producing an abundant supply of food and other products. When improperly managed, however, farms can drain soil nutrients and contaminate the watershed. Through the use of GPS and yield monitors, precision agriculture can mitigate such negative environmental effects by allowing farmers to precisely measure and monitor production. Computer-driven equipment customises irrigation fertiliser application rates according to the needs of the soil and crop in a specific portion of a field (Figure 1). Though precision agriculture promises to improve the sustainability of crop production, such sustainable technologies have not been applied to the livestock sector. Livestock farms in the United States are becoming increasingly large and concentrated — transitioning from traditional farms to confined animal feeding operations (or CAFOs). As of 2010, five per cent of conventional farms raise eighty-five per cent of the grain-fed cattle in America. It is not uncommon for a single CAFO to generate the same amount of waste as a city of 100,000 people. The waste is often left untreated to sit in barns or large lagoons before being sprayed or spread on adjacent fields, where it can

runoff and contaminate nearby streams and waterbodies. How might nascent technologies, like those employed in precision agriculture, help define a sustainable, humane alternative to the CAFO system?

This project does just that by investigating the potential for data driven livestock ranching in the Great Plains (Figure 2). Much of the native grasslands in the Great Plains has been lost to irrigated agriculture. However, research organisations like the Leopold Center for Sustainable Agriculture have advocated for the conversion of ten per cent of cropland to native prairie grass strips in order to mitigate soil erosion and water contamination. We propose a modern cattle drive that would move through these recently converted prairie strips in agricultural lands across the Great Plains.

Mirroring the cattle drive that took place in the same region 120 years ago, the cattle drive of today would employ satellite imagery, remote sensing, drone compatibility, handheld tablets, virtual fencing and cow activity trackers, or CowBits (Figure 3). Geospatial data sets and aerial overlays help calculate path suitability, while drones, virtual fencing and activity trackers help to direct the movement of the herd (Figure 4). Much of the Great Plains has been fragmented by fences, but virtual fencing would allow these scars on the landscape to heal. Wearable technologies also monitor the health and wellness of each animal, as cattle are tracked by movement, health and happiness (Figure 5). With the combinations of such technologies, we propose a matrix that would restore thousands of acres of prairie across the Great Plains and, in so doing, develop a new model for sustainable, responsive livestock production.

Opposite:
Figure 3.
Cattle drive components

Figure 4.
Virtual fencing

Following pages:
Figure 5.
Hereford herd with CowBits

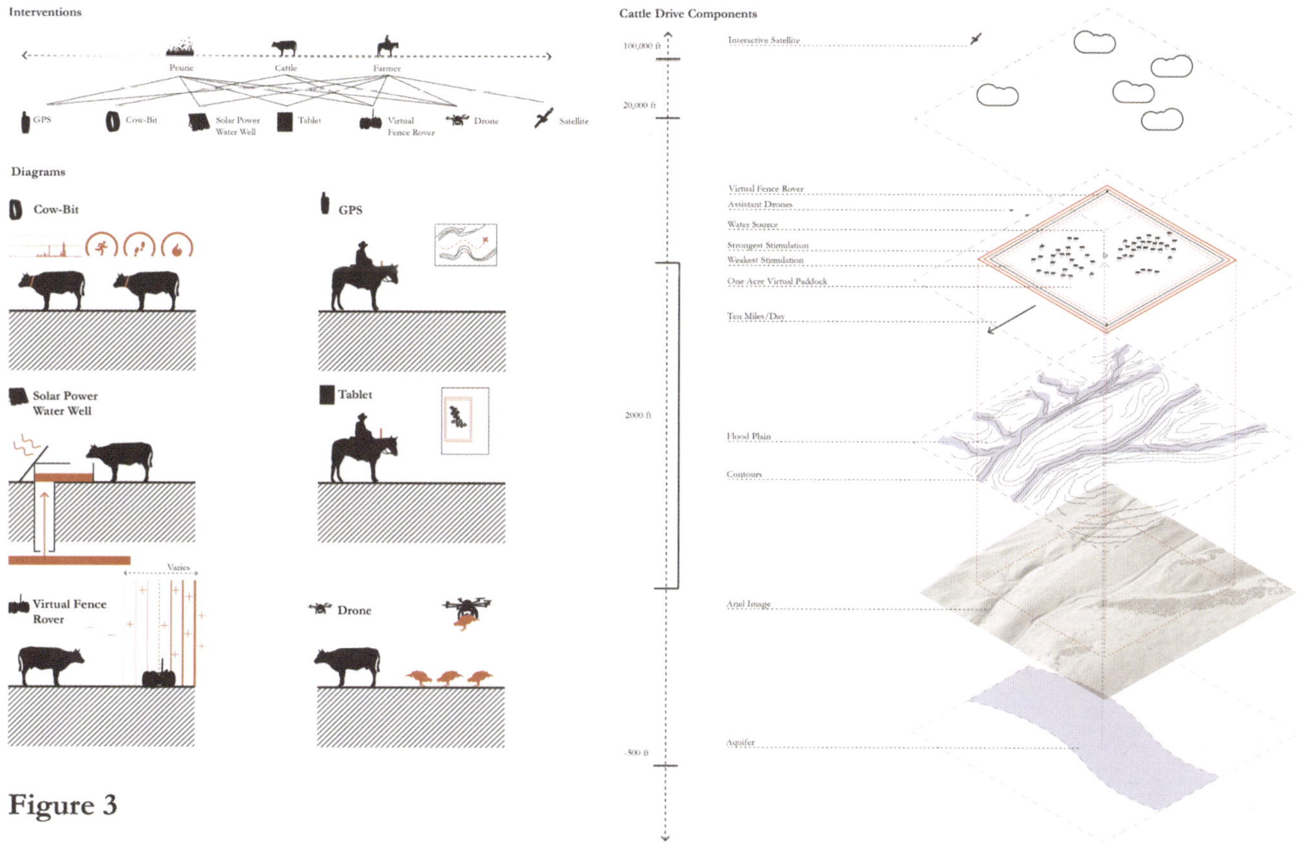

Figure 3

Figure 4

Figure 5

Sensor Drone
92%
89%

'STAGING' NATURE IN THE MUNDANE CITY

Usue Ruiz-Arana

A DIGITAL INSTALLATION FOR THE LANDSCAPE, WILDERNESS, AND THE WILD

Urban citizens frequently ignore the physical environment through which they move on their daily routines. This installation was developed for the 'Landscape, Wilderness and the Wild' conference at Newcastle University. It proposed a digital wilderness as a way to engage with the mundane city and introduce a new aesthetic and relationship with wildlife within the urban realm. The installation took place in the evening at an underused space within the campus and provided a multi-sensory experience to participants engaging sight, sound and smell.

The wilderness presented within took its cue from the 'New Wilderness' that has arisen spontaneously on the former industrial sites at the mouth of the River Tyne. Wild animals, such as foxes, found in these wildernesses bring a need to redefine the relationship between people and wildlife in the urban realm. These sites are often seen as a sign of decline, and increase anxiety caused by fear of crime, but if accepted, could provide direct contact with nature at the heart of the city.

The installation featured a six-minute-long projection onto a stone clad wall, accompanied by an animal soundtrack and the smell of grass and forest. The projection was on a loop for the duration of the installation and imagined how that wall would weather if we let it be. Over time, the natural environment would act upon its surface. Slowly, it would become wilder, until we no longer recognise it as a wall. In this imaginary scenario, the wall became the ground, capable of supporting life, and the setting for wild animals in the city.

This digital intervention successfully brought to life a mundane space within the city, questioned the relationship between people and the wild, and presented wilderness as an escape window to our daily routines, a moral counter-world to its cultural surroundings.

••

Video 01: The video projected during the installation can be viewed at: https://vimeo.com/120165705 (password #percyquad)

Video 02: A video recorded of the projection can be viewed at: https://vimeo.com/123677599 (password #percyquad)

••

1. Bull, M., 2012. The audio-visual iPod. In J. Sterne, ed. The Sound Studies Reader. New York: Routledge.

2. Kowarik, I., 2005. Wild Urban Woodlands: Towards a Conceptual Framework. In I. Kowarik & S. Körner, eds. Wild Urban Woodlands SE - 1. Springer Berlin Heidelberg, pp. 1–32. Available at: http://dx.doi.org/10.1007/3-540-26859-6_1.

3. James, P. et al., 2009. Towards an integrated understanding of green space in the European built environment. Urban Forestry & Urban Greening, 8(2), pp.65–75. Available at: http://linkinghub.elsevier.com/retrieve/pii/S1618866709000144 [Accessed December 3, 2014].

4. Bixler, R.D. & Floyd, M.F., 1997. Nature is Scary, Disgusting, and Uncomfortable. Environment and Behavior, 29, pp.443-467.

5. Kirchhoff, T. & Vicenzotti, V., 2015. 'Wilderness - A Moral Counter World A Typology of European Perceptions of Wild Nature'. Paper presented at the Landscape, Wilderness and the Wild Conference, Newcastle upon Tyne, UK.

Above:
Installation space and
projection wall.

Right:
Participants in installation.

Below:
Presoaked block concealed
in container.

Opposite:
Enjoying the show.

Augmenting XYZRGB: design and the reality captured landscape

Ervine Lin
Yazid Ninsalam
Michaela F. Prescott

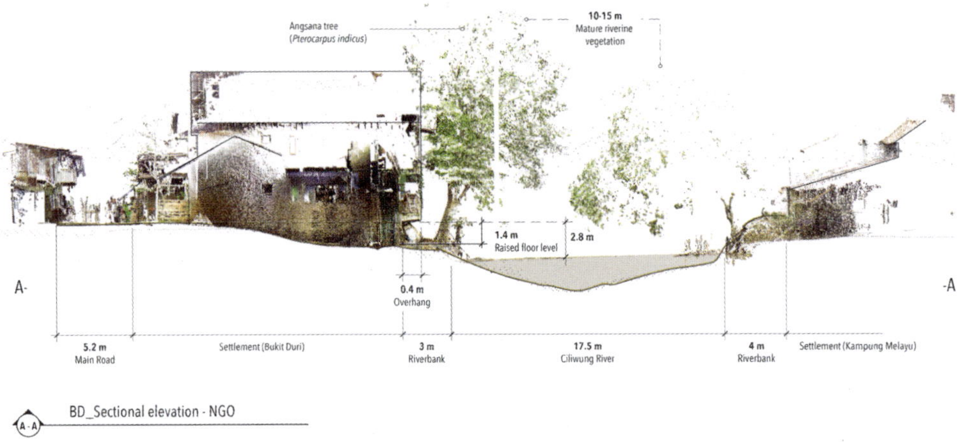

Figure 1:
Cross-section annotated with information collected during local resident interviews and measurements based on point cloud obtained using a terrestrial laser scanner.

Landscape architects are progressively grappling with more complex site issues and the digital realm facilitates access to landscapes that are increasingly vulnerable, with complex site conditions and webs of stakeholders. Through the development of a series of tools and workflows, we are investigating the possibilities of applying landscape architectural ideas to the flood-prone and degraded Ciliwung River, which bisects Jakarta, Indonesia.

We position ourselves between the clinically-precise description of the landscape provided by surveyors and the loose-reality of hyper-landscapes created by the designer. Our data-capture-driven research method relies on the curation of both analogue and digital acquisition techniques. Extensive field interviews and studio-driven measured drawing methods focus on the understanding of the cross-sectional relationship of the river landscape to the urban site. Precision laser-scanned datasets and close-range photogrammetry captured spatial information are geographically referenced within UAV derived point clouds. From these various acquisition techniques we geographically nest the information collected as point clouds into a single digital 3D environment.

These digital doppelgängers are semantically classified to decode in situ landscape elements for further design action. Vegetation and topographical elements can be isolated from the buildings found on site, using height and colour information which is decoded from the massive point cloud data and studied alongside results from interviews with community leaders and residents. Simultaneously, information collected during interviews with local residents is embedded into the digital point cloud cross-sections (Figure 1). The scale and resolution of information gathered is then clarified through the diverse potential use of the dataset for design purposes.

Collecting, digitally revisiting and decoding these reality- sourced point cloud models is the first descriptive step which paves the way for a prescriptive

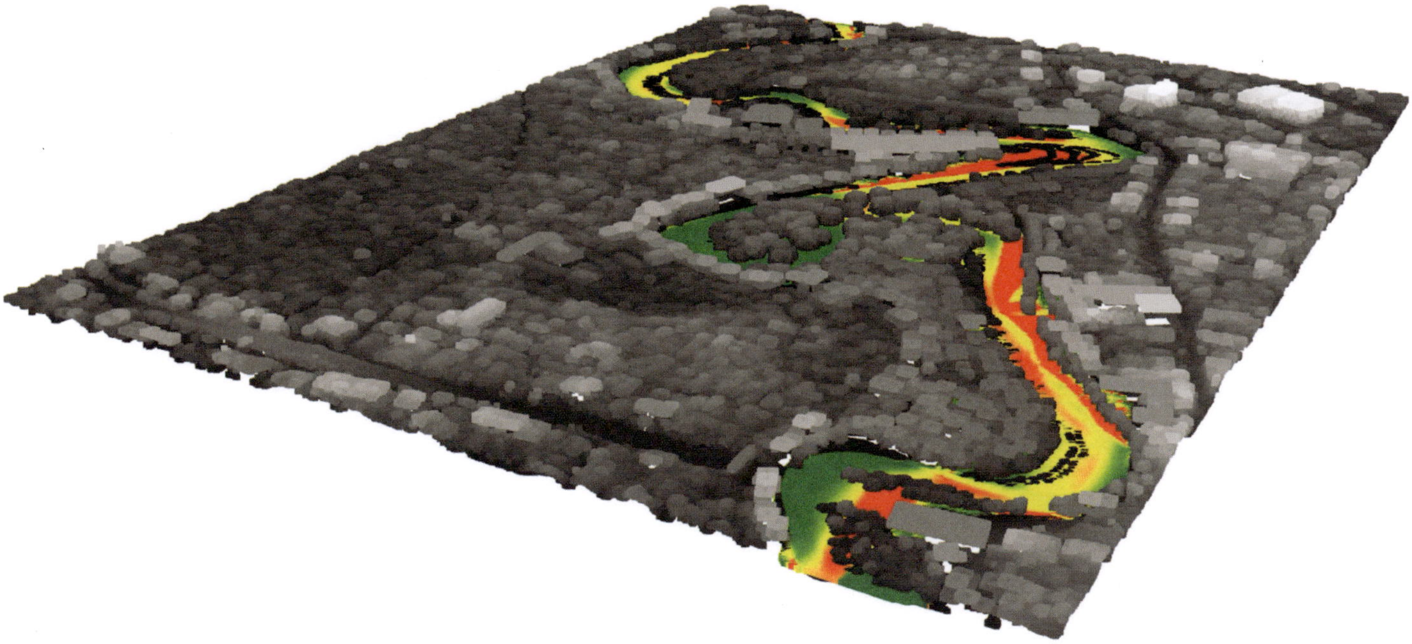

Figure 2:
Flood simulation results can be imported back into the 3D environment to visually study them.

step in which informed interventions can be embedded back into the model. To do this we created a comprehensive set of tools which are able to assist in the modification of the underlying point cloud model, the representation of designed interventions in a point cloud format and the ability to feed these interventions into qualitative models. Being able to cut into and replace existing points with those that are user-generated opens up the possibility of embedding flood mitigation and design scenarios directly into the 3D geo-referenced context ready to be evaluated through hydrodynamic simulations.

With the help of the team's hydraulic engineers, we integrate these scenarios with advanced hydrodynamic simulations to test the efficacy of our designs (Figure 2). Changes in the bathymetry, riparian vegetative cover and course of the river can all be taken into account. The results of the flooding simulations are then projected back into the underlying 3D point cloud model for further analysis. This allows us to step away from the trapezoidal cross section, often used in the design of channel conveyance, towards one which looks to a more sensitive approach using vegetation and topography. As such, addressing not only the immediate issue of flooding, but extending to ideas of ecology, land use, and culture and society.

The tools and methods developed within this case study show potential value for other increasingly vulnerable and complex sites. This approach is, however, not without its challenges, which include managing the increasingly complex information gathered from the site. Additionally, the implementation of the results of this study is confronted by the speed of change within a developing city, such as Jakarta, and the numerous stakeholders involved. At present, the promising results obtained — which provide designers greater insight into the workings of a complex site — demonstrate unprecedented rigour in both the understanding and spatial representation of urban landscape challenges.

ARTIST PROFILE
:
ELISE MC CURLEY

INTO THE BLUE

Into the Blue is a video art installation for a Master of Fine Arts video studio.

The content of the film was inspired by the emotive phenomena of sound and the influence of invisible forces on the physical body. The piece is also inspired by the architectural installation entitled Apparition, by Antoine Predock, as part of the Warming Hut competition.

The film is the narrative of a character influenced and affected by the invisible forces surrounding her. The fragmentation of the film is the visible interpretation of the effect of the environment on the character.

Sound and image interact in unexpected ways, creating the place and narrative for the installation. Generative image manipulation was used to create the 'Digital Landscape' for the artwork.

Stream online link: https://vimeo.com/112873807

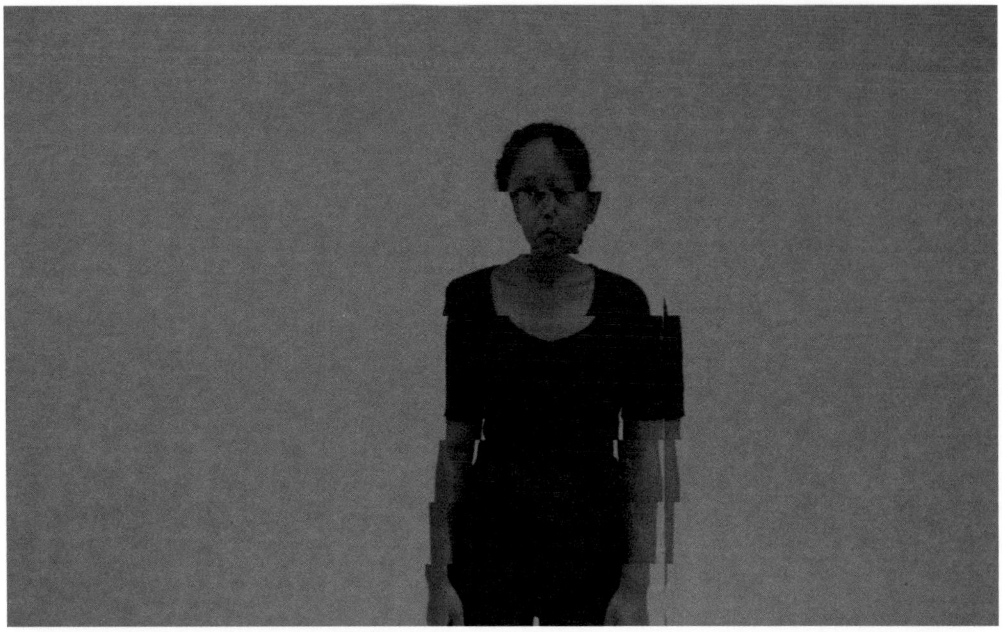

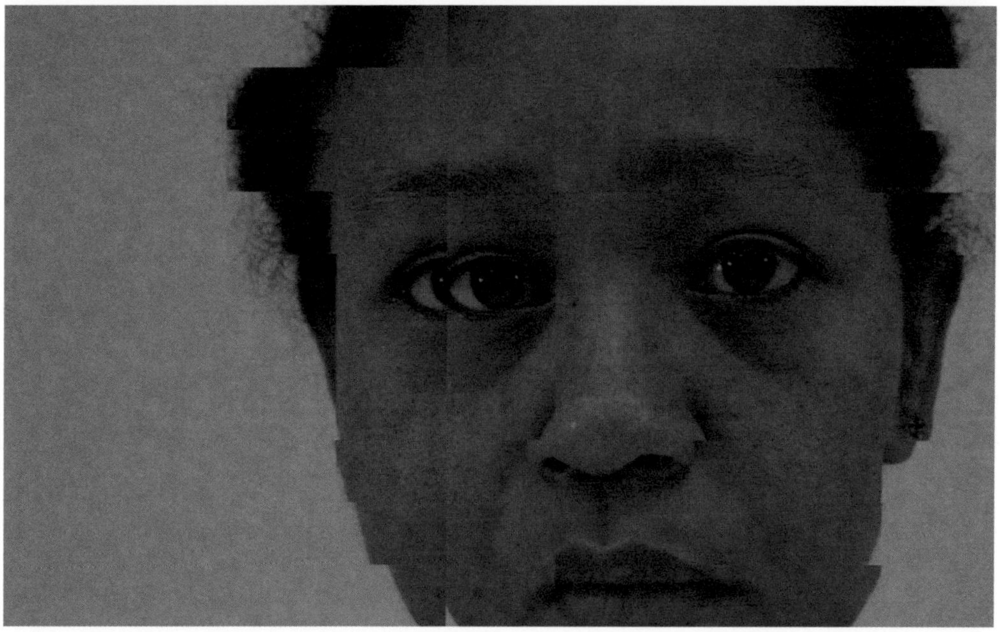

Project

Flash floods and desert claims

Christophe Girot
Philipp RW Urech

THE ARCHITECTURE OF NEW RESILIENT SETTLEMENTS IN THE SONORAN DESERT OF ARIZONA

The ETH Zürich Landscape Modelling and Visualising Studio investigated future scenarios for water-restrained settlements in the Sonoran Desert of Arizona, near the US/Mexico border. It primarily addressed the challenge of large-scale landscape urban design in an area southwest of the city of Tucson prone to flash floods and severe erosion. The students were asked to study and manipulate the local topography to enable the retention of flood waters for seasonal settlement and periodic cultivation. The combination of an architectural and landscape architectural approach were integrated at different scales in a model generating a broad range of topological possibilities, solutions and visions for potential settlements in the future. A field trip to Arizona was undertaken with 20 ETH students, together with 12 students from the Technical University in Delft, to gain a precise insight into the situation at hand, combining site expeditions, presentations and workshops with group discussions.

The studio focused on the dynamics of water systems and the development of a holistic design approach integrating topography, vegetation and human settlement and activities. Back at ETH, sand modelling, CNC prototyping and visualisation techniques were successively taught to students in a series of workshops in order to develop tangible and precise landscape structures at various scales and stages of development. New means of digital landscape representation were developed allowing for new landscape typologies to emerge both spatially and in terms of program and use. The students worked on site-specific strategies using 3D geographically-positioned models based on Lidar data delivered to us by the Pima county authorities, which enabled them to take into account the amplitude and dynamics of floods in relation to terrain, topography, vegetation and settlement. Analogue tools (sketches, sections, models and plans) were used and combined alternately with computer tools (CNC modelling, computer analysis and 3D visualisation) to help define and implement accurate new topologies in the landscape. With the newly gained skills in CAD/CAM for CNC modelling, ETH students were able to topographically develop the design of the landscape as a response to site conditions.

The goal of the studio was to develop a set of varying landscape approaches to a given site. ETH students were asked to imagine how people could better live in this very dry and hot landscape, prone to flash floods in the summer, yet respect an integral part of the American Southwest desert culture. The studio goal was achieved by digitally adapting architectural and landscape architectural approaches to questions of topography, water dynamics, vegetation and settlement patterns. It resulted in a landscape project acting as a single whole, by combining advanced means of modelling and representation with regard to fluctuating water runoff. It has helped locate, scale and define entirely new development strategies for the Sonoran Desert.

Opposite:
ETH Digital Model image of a plan of new settlement alongside washes in the Altar Valley.
Wieland Schwarz, Guillaume Guisan

Above and following pages:
ETH Digital model image showing perspective section through the new settlement.

Opposite:
ETH Ditigal model image showing a detail view of housing for a desert research center in the Sonoran landscape.
Tania Depallens, David Häusler

Opposite:
ETH Digital model image showing the proposal of a new urban and agricultural development in the lower Altar Valley.
Coralie Berchtold, Karoline Heene, Tanja Vallaster

Right:
ETH Digital model image bird's-eye view of a weir system to spread flood water in the Altar Valley.
Stéphanie Chanson, Andrea Micanovic

Abram Ebersohn & Greg Dahlke

Abram Ebersohn and Greg Dahlke are in their last semester of undergraduate at the LSU Robert Reich School of Landscape Architecture. Abram has a strong affection for the environment and landscape architecture helped to guide that passion. He is anxious but more excited to see on what journey the skills, passion, and knowledge he has learned from studying landscape architecture will eventually lead him. Greg will be spending 27 months in Senegal with the Peace Corps to create more sustainable agriculture system, understand the importance of food and people, and absorb all the surrounding information. Afterward, he intends to further explore how landscape architecture and agriculture can improve and develop together.

Bradley Cantrell

Bradley Cantrell is an associate professor at the Harvard Graduate School of Design and design researcher at Invivia whose work focuses on the role of computation and media in environmental and ecological design. Professor Cantrell received his BSLA from the University of Kentucky and his MLA from the Harvard Graduate School of Design. He is the author of the ASLA award-winning book Digital Drawing for Landscape Architecture, Modeling the Environment, and Responsive Landscapes, forthcoming 2015.

David Mah

David Mah has been a lecturer at Harvard's Graduate School of Design since 2010. Previous to Harvard, he has taught at Cornell University's departments of Architecture as well as City and Regional Planning from 2007 till 2010. David has also taught design studio within the postgraduate design, Landscape Urbanism program at the Architectural Association in London from 2004 till 2007 and has conducted design workshops at the Peking University's Graduate School of Landscape Architecture in China and Konkuk University in Korea. David has worked within a number of international design practices including FOA and Zaha Hadid Architects where he was engaged in the design and delivery of a number of large landscape and masterplanning as well as architectural projects in the United Kingdom, Singapore and Spain.

www.asensio-mah.com

Ann Marie Schneider

Currently a Landscape Designer at Walker Macy, Ann Marie Schneider holds degrees from the University of Pennsylvania, The School of the Art Institute of Chicago, Archeworks and the LCC Media Institute of Photography. In contrast to her creative education, she has over a decade of professional experience as a technology consultant in Chicago, London and Sydney for global financial institutions. In pursuit of reconciling her experience in technology, with her education and practice in visual arts, she chose PennDesign's cross-disciplinary program to obtain her Masters degree in Landscape Architecture and Regional Planning. She is currently working on the Portage Bay Park design and the Lake2Bay corridor project in Seattle while continuing to explore data visualization's potential for the practice of art and design.

Brian Davis

Brian Davis (@faslanyc) is an assistant professor of landscape architecture at Cornell University. He teaches design studios as well as classes on construction technology and Latin American landscapes. He also founded and directs the Landscape Change Lab at Cornell University. His research looks at the relationship between landscapes and instruments with a particular geographic focus in Latin America and New York State, and is organized through the Borderlands

Dongsei Kim

Dongsei Kim is an architect, urbanist, and educator. He is an Assistant Professor at Korea University, and a PhD candidate at the University of Melbourne. He has extensive international teaching experience including Columbia, Carleton, RMIT, Monash, VUW, and Kyunghee Universities. He received his MDesS with distinction from Harvard University, MSAUD from Columbia University, and a B.Arch (Hons) from VUW. His work interrogates how nation-state borders influence spatial inclusion and exclusion across scales. His Korean Demilitarized Zone research was exhibited in the recent Golden Lion Award winning Korean Pavilion at the 14th Venice Architecture Biennale and published in journals and books.

ATLAS Lab

ATLAS Lab is a design and research lab founded by Kimberly Garza and Andrew tenBrink. The lab is centered on the pairing of art and ecology to create toolsets that empower the urban realm. The design interventions ATLAS produces seeks to impact cities in two ways: through the injection of art and play in the everyday urban experience, and the integration of ecology in the urban environment. Whether a small-scale urban installation or large-scale master plan, design interventions are guided by a rigorous research process to develop strategies that are historically, culturally and socially responsive.

Eduardo Rico

Eduardo Rico is a Civil Engineer and Ma Landscape Urbanism Graduate currently working in Arup, as well as member of design practices such as Groundlab and Relational Urbanism. He is currently engaged in strategic advice on infrastructure and transportation for urban master planning in the ILG team in Arup. Eduardo focuses his work and research in alternative design practices which feed infrastructural inputs into architectural urbanism. He has been co director with Enriqueta Llabres of the Relational Urbanism Studio in Berlage Institute 2010 and 2012 as well as GSD Harvard 2013. Eduardo is currently co director of the Ma Landscape Urbanism in the Architectural association. Eduardo Rico has extensively lectured on his work on Infrastructures and Landscape as well contributed to various articles and books on the subject matter.

Elise McCurley

Elise McCurley is an architect, designer and artist. She holds degrees in architecture from California Polytechnic University, San Luis Obispo and University of Pennsylvania (UPenn) with additional studies completed in the Fine Arts department at UPenn, earning a certificate in Interactive and Time Based Media. Elise is most interested in developing projects combining and/or intersecting art, architecture, and landscape architecture. Much of her work focuses on the translations of environments into various media by using digital tools in a meaningful method tied to analysis and data driven processes.

Gaia Scagnetti

Dr. Gaia Scagnetti is an expert in Visual Epistemology as well as Information Visualization and Mapping. Her current research investigates the impact of Information Visualization on design discourse with a focus on design education.

At present she is full-time Assistant Professor at the Pratt Institute's Graduate Communications department in New York.

In 2010 Gaia Scagnetti completed a Post Doctoral research at the Design Lab at the Massachusetts Institute of Technology.

As Researcher and Design Strategist at MIT she conducted qualitative research for design in the topic of social sustainability, connectivity and mobility. In 2009 she obtained a PhD degree cum Meritus in Industrial Design and Multimedia Communication at the Politecnico di Milano. During her doctoral research Gaia worked as a designer and researcher at the DensityDesignLab in Milan, where she carried out research, design projects and teaching activities on Information Visualization and Mapping.

Her works have been featured in several conferences and exhibitions (DesignEd, HyperUrbain.2, the MIT Humanities + Digital Conference, NetSci2010 - Arts | Humanities | Complex Networks, SIGGRAPH09 Emerging technology Conference, the MediaLAB Prado - Visualizar08) and publications and showcases (DataFlow 2, VisualComplexity.com, Mapping pattern of information, Malofiej 19, Visual storytelling, Parson Journal of Information Mapping). Her complete portfolio can be found at www.namedgaia.com.

Jung Hyun-Woo

Junghyun Woo completed the advanced Master of architecture at Berlage Institute in Rotterdam. She practiced at Relational Urbanism Office in London, MVRDV in Rotterdam, and previously worked for SIAPLAN in Seoul. She lectured and was invited as a guest critic at various universities in South Korea, US, and the Netherlands. She visited at Taliesin, as the visiting architect and guest critic in 2012. She taught Relational Urbanism Studio as the instructor at the Berlage in TU Delft from 2012 to 2013. She received research fellowship for the transportation and public infrastructure from Perkins Eastman office in New York 2015. Now she is researching the topic related to infrastructure, logistics and economies associated with Ocean environments at Harvard Graduate School of Design.

Elle Stephenson

Currently in her 4th year of a Bachelor of Visual Arts/Bachelor of Arts at Monash University. Her interest and practice lies in tracking human movement. That is, in a world of mass production, anonymous spectacle and sterile surface it has become increasingly difficult to leave a trace. As a pursuit to find a solution, her experiments act as surrogates and maps of existence. Her work explores the fusion between installation practice, video work, digital representations and drawing. More specifically, a preoccupation with digital and filmic explorations derives from her Arts major in Film Studies.

Jack Isles

Jack Isles is an Architecture graduate based in Melbourne Australia. He received his BArch (Dist) from the Royal Melbourne Institute of Technology. Jack's ongoing work interrogates the political and economic systems that define architecture at a local and territorial scale. Through his research he has acted as teaching assistant in design studios at RMIT on the contested borders of the South China Sea. His ongoing work on the Korean Peninsula's demilitarized zone has been exhibited alongside colleague Dongsei Kim at DNA Gallery in Berlin, whilst Jack's research to be published in 2015 discusses how landscape architecture has become central to the geopolitics of claiming sovereignty. Jack has travelled extensively across South America and his ongoing research engages the dynamic and fluid socio/economic landscape of the Latin

Justine Holzman

Justine Holzman is a landscape researcher and visiting assistant professor at The Robert Reich School of Landscape Architecture at Louisiana State University. She received a BA in Landscape Architecture from the University of California Berkeley and an MLA from the Robert Reich School of Landscape Architecture. Her current research recognizes the inherent responsive capabilities of landscape through its materiality and her work in ceramics and digital fabrication has been exhibited across the United States. She is the author of Responsive Landscapes, forthcoming 2015.

Enriqueta Llabres

Enriqueta Llabres is an architect graduated in Barcelona (2002) with a Master in Science in Local Economic Development from The London School of Economics (2011) Between 2003 and 2007 she worked for the ETH Professor Josep Lluis Mateo, contributing to emblematic projects of the firm such as the Catalonian Film Theatre. In 2007 she moved to London founding Relational Urbanism. She is currently a Design Critic in Landscape Architecture in Harvard Graduate School of Design and has directed with Eduardo Rico the Relational Urbanism Design Studio at the Berlage Institute between 2011 and 2013. She has collaborated with a wide number of institutions worldwide as design critic, lecturer and visiting lecturer.

Joe W.T. Scott

Joe W.T. Scott is British born, Melbourne based writer. He specialises in the fields of art criticism, interviews, blogging, copywriting and online content. In 2012 Joe gained his Bachelor of Arts from The University of Melbourne with a double major in literature and art history. He also exhibited art projects at Kings ARI, SEVENTH Gallery and Mudfest. In 2013 he completed further study in art history for which he was awarded first class honours. His thesis explored the work of Swiss contemporary artist Thomas Hirschhorn. In 2014 Joe produced written work for numerous publications, galleries and artists including Daine Singer, SEVENTH Gallery, Next Wave Festival, Dispatch and Silver Lane Studio creative agency. In 2015 Joe has so far spoken at the Digital Writers Festival and is set to commence a number of new writing projects later in the year. He regularly posts on his blog which contains essays, journals, interviews, reviews, videos and more.

Minimaforms

Brothers Stephen and Theodore Spyropoulos founded Minimaforms in 2002. Their work is in the permanent collections of the FRAC Centre, the Signum Foundation and the Archigram Archive. Recent exhibitions have included work shown at the Museum of Modern Art, Barbican Centre, Detroit Institute of Arts, ICA, FRAC Centre amongst others. Recent projects include two thematic pier landmarks and the illumination concept for a Renzo Piano's master planned 760-acre National Park in Athens, a large-scale land art work in Norway, and Nesta commission on behavioral robotics. Theodore Spyropoulos is an architect and educator. He is the Director of the Architectural Association's world renowned Design Research Lab (AADRL) in London. In 2013 the Association for Computer-Aided Design in Architecture awarded him The ACADIA award of excellence for his educational work directing the AADRL. Stephen Spyropoulos is an artist and interactive designer. He is the head of user experience and design for Gilt Groupe and has also been the design director for Heavy, and a faculty member at Rutgers School of Art teaching interactive design.

Nadia Amoroso

Nadia Amoroso, PhD, ASLA, is an academic in Landscape Architecture and Urban Design. Her work focuses on visual representation, urban design and creative mapping. She is a GeoDesign and Creative Cartography Evangelist. She teaches at the University of Guelph, Department of Landscape Architecture and operates a landscape architectural design and visualization practice in Toronto, Canada. She is the author/ editor of a number of books including, The Exposed City: Mapping the Urban Invisibles, Representing Landscapes: A Visual Collection of Landscape Architectural Drawings, Digital Landscape Architecture Now and more recently Representing Landscapes: Digital. She has a BLA and MUD from John H. Daniels Faculty of Architecture, Landscape, and Design also at the University of Toronto and a PhD from the Bartlett School of Architecture.

www.nadiaamoroso.com

Rosalea Monacella

Rosalea's teaching focuses and builds on an integrated scholarship model, where teaching design, research seminars and theoretical frameworks course directly draw on her research expertise, exploring and sharing a number of the research thematics and approaches in the teaching curriculum and pedagogical structure. Rosalea has been a recipient of a number of national and international awards related to her research undertakings. The OUTR lab, which she co-directs, has undertaken research on a number of cities around the world and completed a number of urban masterplans in China, USA, South America, Europe and Australia that explores design at the nexus of the urban and natural environments. The approach is for the generation of sustainable urban futures for living through a practice of design that is informed from the 'ground-up & top down forces' through a careful and rigorous exploration of economic, environmental, and social complex systems that constitute an ever-changing city. The research brings together complex urban issues and advanced digital modelling techniques as an approach for providing solutions. Rose brings a deep knowledge and expertise in transforming the urban environment and the impact of the shifting dynamics in resource flows. This can be evidenced through her experience- www.outr.org

Usue Ruiz-Arana

I am a PhD researcher at Newcastle University and associate landscape architect for a british studio, OOBE Ltd. My research explores the 'staging' of nature in the everyday spaces of the city through multisensorial interventions that seek to engage with those spaces, introduce a new landscape aesthetic and relationship with the wild within the urban realm, and unfold the perception of nature through the different senses.

Phillipp Rw Urech

Philipp R.W. Urech, born in Vevey (CH), studied architecture at the Academy of Architecture (USI) in Mendrisio and at the Swiss Federal Institute of Technology (ETH) in Zürich where he graduated in 2009 at the chair of Prof. Deplazes. Since 2009 he is collaborator at the office S+M Dello Buono Architekten in Zürich where he participated in developing numerous building submissions, planning studies and competitions. Since 2010 he works as a teaching assistent at the chair of Landscape Architecture of Prof. Christophe Girot at the ETH (Swiss Federal Institute of Technology) in Zürich. He taught in several Design studios, Theses electives and Master thesis projects. Design research studies include the Rhine-Meuse Delta in Dordrecht (NL), the Ciliwung River in Jakarta, Indonesia, and the Sonoran Desert in Arizona.

Nadia D'Agnone

Nadia D'Agnone is a Landscape Architectural Designer and Researcher. She was born in Toronto, Canada and is now based in Venice, Italy where she is completing her Ph.D. research at the Università Iuav di Venezia. She has an Honours Bachelor of Arts from the University of Toronto in Fine Art Visual Studies and Architectural Studies and a Master of Landscape Architecture from the John H. Daniels Faculty of Architecture, Landscape, and Design also at the University of Toronto. Her interests lie in exploring the interdisciplinary relationships between design, art, philosophy, and science through exploratory techniques in visual communication including creative mapping, modeling and data visualization.

Sha Hwang

Sha Hwang is an information designer and technologist based mostly in Brooklyn. A failed architect and an accidental entrepreneur, Sha has designed and built work for clients such as the New York Times, the Harvard Library, CNN, MTV, Flickr, and Adobe. Previously, Sha worked at

Stamen Design and later cofounded the company Movity, which was acquired by the real estate company Trulia. Sha has also spent time exploring his interests in fabrication and digital art in projects like Meshu and Gifpop. In 2013, Sha was called in as a part of the tech surge team to help redesign Healthcare.gov, and has since cofounded Nava to continue to improve government digital services.

Janet Laurence

Exploring notions of art, science, imagination, memory, and loss, Janet Laurence's practice examines the interconnection of life forms and ecologies and observes the impact that humans have on the threatened, natural world. Laurence's work addresses our relationship to nature through both site specific and gallery works. Experimenting with and working in varying mediums, Laurence continues to create immersive environments that navigate the interconnections between all living forms. Her practice has sustained organic qualities and a sense of transience, occupying the liminal zones, or places where art, science, imagination and memory converge.

Christophe Girot

Christophe Girot is Full Professor and Chair of Landscape Architecture at the Architecture

Department of the ETH in Zürich. His teaching and research interest span over the following three themes:

New topological methods in landscape design.

Landscape perception and analysis through new media.

Contemporary theory and history of landscape architecture. His professional practice is focused on large-scale landscape projects, which contribute to sustainable urban environments.

PEG Office

PEG office of landscape + architecture, co-founded by Karen M'Closkey and Keith VanDerSys, is an award-winning design and research office based in Philadelphia, Pennsylvania. PEG's work explores the potential for new media and fabrication technologies to produce novel relationships between organic and inorganic materials, often utilizing pattern as a means to heighten the perception of temporal and ephemeral phenomena. Established in 2004, PEG has been published internationally and won numerous design awards, including the 2010 Emerging New York Architects prize, 2010 Architectural League Prize for Young Architects and Designers, 2013 PEW Fellowship in the Arts, and was recently named to the "Select Ten" list of thought leaders in design by Metropolis Magazine. PEG recently organized the Simulating Natures symposium at the University of Pennsylvania and will be guest editing the upcoming issue of LA+ Simulation around the same theme. They are also co-authoring the forthcoming book Dynamic Patterns: Visualizing Landscapes in a Digital Age.

Thomas Mical

Thomas Mical is Associate Professor of Architectural Theory at the University of South Australia. He does research on stealth landscapes, and the curios intersections of architectural theory with media-philosophy, especially around questions of presence and absence.Thomas Mical is Associate Professor of Architectural Theory at the University of South Australia. He does research on stealth landscapes, and the curios intersections of architectural theory with media-philosophy, especially around questions of presence and absence.

Rod Barnett

Barnett comes to WUSTL from Auburn University in Alabama, where he is chair of the Graduate Program in Landscape Architecture. He previously taught at the Unitec Institute of Technology in Auckland, New Zealand, and directed the Unitec Landscape Unit, the Department of Landscape Architecture's research wing. In 2012, DesignIntelligence named him one of its 25 most admired educators.

Barnett has written extensively on nonlinear landscape architecture and received grants from both arts and science organizations to pursue this interest in a variety of design contexts. His private practice has focused on gardens, which allow him to explore the fluid and interactive connections between humans and their personal environments.

Michaela Prescott

Michaela F. Prescott is a researcher in the Landscape Ecology module at the Future Cities Laboratory, Singapore. This position includes a Ph.D. candidature in Architecture under the ETH Zurich, Switzerland. Prior to this she completed a Master in Landscape Architecture and a Bachelor of Design at the Royal Melbourne Institute of Technology in Melbourne, Australia. Her research investigates the use of site specific socio-cultural knowledge to derive spatial parameters for the design of riverine landscapes in Indonesia.

Yazid Ninsalam

Yazid Ninsalam is a doctoral candidate at the National University of Singapore and a researcher at Future Cities Laboratory. He graduated with honours in Bachelor of Arts (Architecture) before gaining a Master in Landscape Architecture at the National University of Singapore. In his research he investigates the use of reality captured information for landscape architecture design action. His focus on close-range digital reconstruction of urban landscapes has warranted work in diverse sites such as Mumbai, Manila, Bali, Jakarta, and Singapore.

Ervine Lin

Ervine Lin is a researcher in the Landscape Ecology module at the Future Cities Laboratory (FCL), a project of the Singapore ETH Centre (SEC), Singapore. He is currently a PhD candidate with the ETH Zurich after completing his Master of Landscape Architecture with the National University of Singapore. His research revolves around enabling designers and planners to use reality captured point cloud data to visualise and more importantly predict the resultant impacts of large scale interventions on the landscape.

Advertising and Sponsorship

The **Kerb** production team and the RMIT Landscape Architecture program would like to thank our sponsors for their generous financial support toward this not-for-profit publication.

••

RMIT Architecture and Design

••

PATRON

Taylor Cullity Lethlean

T.C.L

LANDSCAPE ARCHITECTURE
URBAN DESIGN

••

FRIENDS

Sue Barnsley Design

Enlocus

Hansen Partnership